AMERICAN COMMODITIES IN AN AGE OF EMPIRE

AMERICAN COMMODITIES
IN AN AGE OF EMPIRE

MONA DOMOSH

Routledge
Taylor & Francis Group
New York   London

Routledge is an imprint of the
Taylor & Francis Group, an informa business

Published in 2006 by
Routledge
Taylor & Francis Group
270 Madison Avenue
New York, NY 10016

© 2006 by Taylor & Francis Group, LLC
Routledge is an imprint of Taylor & Francis Group

Printed in the United States of America on acid-free paper
10 9 8 7 6 5 4 3 2 1

International Standard Book Number-10: 0-415-94571-2 (Hardcover) 0-415-94572-0 (Softcover)
International Standard Book Number-13: 978-0-415-94571-4 (Hardcover) 978-0-415-94572-1 (Softcover)

Library of Congress Cataloging-in-Publication Data

Domosh, Mona, 1957-
American commodities in an age of empire / by Mona Domosh.
    p. cm.
Includes bibliographical references and index.
1. United States--Foreign economic relations. 2. National
characteristics, American. 3. United States--Civilization. 4.
Imperialism--History. I. Title.

HF1455.D66 2006
337.73--dc22   2005034043

Taylor & Francis Group
is the Academic Division of Informa plc.

Visit the Taylor & Francis Web site at
http://www.taylorandfrancis.com

and the Routledge Web site at
http://www.routledge-ny.com

To Frank
for all the harvest moons

Contents

Acknowledgments

Writing this book has been risky business for me. It has forced me to leave the relative comfort of a subfield I know well — urban historical geography — and venture into others where my footing was initially less firm (visual culture, economic history, geopolitics). It also has taken me to unfamiliar terrain: corporate headquarter buildings and for-profit archives, Archangel and Zululand, banquets in Siam, and business deals in Moscow. I couldn't have taken those risks, and had so much fun doing so, without the support and comfort provided by many friends, colleagues, families, and institutions.

I'm always reminded that place really does matter when I walk into my office in the Geography Department at Dartmouth College and feel at home. To everyone who has helped make it that way, I am most grateful. I particularly want to thank Jodie Davi, Ben Forest, Misha, Chris Sneddon, Kelly Woodward, and Richard Wright. Several students participated in this research as Dartmouth Presidential Scholars. I benefited from their insights and from their company: Rachel Abramowitz, Kate Douglas, Lindsay Hirschfeld, Jared Knote, Chelsea Lane-Miller, and Haley Peckett. To the many friends, family members, and colleagues who have offered their comments, thoughts, and general support on various aspects of this book and/or of my life, my heartfelt thanks: Susan Ackerman, Denis Cosgrove, Walter Delaney, Jill Domosh, Felix Driver, Cynthia Enloe, Susanne Freidberg, Gail Hollander, Melissa Hyams, Matthew Frye Jacobson, Irene Kacandes, Wayne LaJoie, Pam Martin, JoBeth Mertens, Peggy Mevs, Catherine Nash, Rod Neumann, Miles Ogborn, Steve Pile, Connie Reimer, Jenny Robinson, Adrian Randolph, Angela Rosenthal, Joni Seager, Richard Sealey, Michael Steinitz, and Sian Steward. As cliché as it might sound, my parents really have always been there for me. Saying thank you barely does justice to what that means.

Many of the ideas in this book were first "aired" as talks that I gave at various institutions and settings: the geography departments at Open University and UCLA, the International Relations department at Florida International University, the London Group of Historical Geographers, the Organization of American Historians conference, and the Association of American Geographers annual conferences. I can't overestimate the importance of these gatherings and the opportunities they provided to discuss my ideas and hear feedback from colleagues. They also made the process of writing this book a little less lonely. I owe particular thanks to John Agnew and an anonymous reviewer, who read the entire manuscript and offered generous comments and suggestions. They forced me to sharpen and clarify some of my arguments, while gently reminding me to let go of others.

I'm particularly appreciative of the following people who provided assistance in sorting through documents and archives and in receiving permissions to use images: Lee Grady at the Wisconsin Historical Society, Raymond Curtin at Eastman Kodak Company, Kathleen Connor at the George Eastman House, Debbie Foster and Judy Henry at H.J. Heinz Company, and Cheryl Chouiniere at The History Factory. I owe a special thanks to Sébastien Caquard, cartographer par excellence, who created such "classic" maps for this book.

I received generous support to conduct this research from the Rockefeller Center/Reiss Family Grant at Dartmouth College and from the National Science Foundation under Grant No. 9911232. Any opinions, findings, and conclusions or recommendations expressed in this material are those of the author and do not necessarily reflect the views of the National Science Foundation. I was also fortunate to be granted a Senior Faculty leave from Dartmouth College that provided a much-needed year away from teaching so that I could focus on writing this manuscript. Portions of chapters 1 and 6 were previously published in "Selling Civilization: Toward a Cultural Analysis of America's Economic Empire in the late 19th and early 20th Centuries," *Transactions of the Institute of British Geographers*, Vol. 29, 2004, pp. 453–467; parts of chapter 1 were published in © 2002 Edward Arnold (Publishers) Ltd. "A 'Civilized' Commerce: Gender, 'Race,' and Empire at the 1893 Chicago Exposition," *Cultural Geographies*, Vol. 9, 2002, pp. 183–203 (www.hodderarnoldjournals.com); and portions of chapter 5 appeared in "Purity and Pickles: Discourses of Food, Empire and Work in Turn-of-the-Century United States," *Journal of Social and Cultural Geography*, Vol. 4, No. 1, 2003, pp. 7–26. I want to thank Blackwell Publishers, Edward Arnold Publishers, and Taylor & Francis, respectively, for granting me permission to reprint some of this work here.

David McBride knew when to nudge me and knew when to leave me alone. He also provided much-needed commentary on a draft of this book at a point when I could barely see it. I couldn't ask for a better editor.

And to Frank, whose ebullience is contagious, I thank you for walking — or perhaps I should say "stalking" — into my life. From the Poly boys to the Hallidays, Lundys, and Magilligans, you've made your family part of mine. How lucky for me.

1

Selling Civilization

Its [the Centennial Exhibition's] object is to bring before the world the resources of the people of our nation in friendly competition with those of other nations. In its results it will test the relative advantage of a government by the people over imperial governments, for the successful development of the great works of peace. The vast preparations being made for our Exhibition by foreign nations realizes to us the necessity of leaving nothing undone which in these respects will determine, on our own soil, our real position of leadership in the world.

— *International Exhibition* (1875)

We need at this juncture to reintroduce the question of diversity in the making of the North American informal empire. In part, this can be accomplished by considering other cultural mediators whose texts and visions have left an important and enduring imprint in the metanarratives of U.S. expansionism.

—Ricardo D. Salvatore, "The Enterprise of Knowledge: Representational Machines of Informal Empire," in *Close Encounters of Empire: Writing the Cultural History of U.S.-Latin American Relations,* ed. Gilbert M. Joseph, Catherine C. Legrand and Ricardo D. Salvatore (Durham: Duke University Press, 1998), 70.

Commercial Geography Lessons

When Mrs. Helen A. Chase of Haverhill, Massachusetts, thumbed through her February 1894 issue of *Ladies' Home Journal* (see Figure 1.1), scanning the various articles, advice columns, and advertisements for hints about how to decorate her home, clothe her family, and prepare dinner that night, she was performing a ritual of middle-class American domesticity that taught her about the world. By 1894, many American companies, particularly those that manufactured mass-produced commodities, were selling their products overseas, and they used this association to the foreign to promote their products at home. In this way, people like Mrs. Chase learned about other peoples and other places. They were participants in an early global worldview, one learned not from the pages of geography textbooks, but from the words and images that filled their magazines and from the commodities that littered their homes, farms, and cities. In this book, I explore some of these commercial geography "lessons" in order to understand how American economic dominance throughout large portions of the world came to be understood by everyday Americans as natural, inevitable, and fundamentally good.

Most "metanarratives" of American expansionism point to the 1898 Spanish-American War as a critical starting point — to the rallying cries of Teddy Roosevelt up San Juan Hill and the acquisition or annexation of the Philippines, Puerto Rico, Guam, and Hawaii.[1]

Figure 1.1   Cover of 1894 issue of *Ladies' Home Journal,* with the following mailing label: Mrs. Helen A. Chase, 4 Maple Ave., Haverhill, MA. (Collection of the author.)

Yet long before military men and machines had reached the shores of other nations, American products — not American guns — were busy "subduing" and "civilizing" the "natives." Since the mid-19th century, the United States had been engaged in what has been called informal imperialism, defined by Mark Crinson as a "form of imperialism by which control was established through ostensibly peaceful means of free trade and economic integration."[2] The ideological configuration of this era of imperialism informed both America's military interventions of the late 19th century and its later economic and cultural dominance over large portions of the world. Central to this configuration was the belief that American economic expansion beyond its national borders was different from, and better than, the military and political maneuvers of imperial Europe. In other words, American commercial expansion was, as the opening quote of this chapter suggests, a great work of peace, a noble cause.

Today, most people would have difficulty taking the sentiments behind this idea seriously. Judging leadership in the world by the "successful development of the great works of peace" would require attention to international aid agencies, health care initiatives, or the number of political and cultural ambassadors. In 1875, however, a very different meaning was at hand: "great works of peace" referred to machines and other industrial commodities, not medical breakthroughs or international governing bodies. This quote was taken from a book published in anticipation of America's Centennial Exhibition, held in Philadelphia in 1876. What was on display there were the products of industrial development — machines and the commodities they made. How and why these things were represented as "works of peace" by companies that sold them overseas, and in what ways this discursive fashioning of commodities as "gifts" constituted and reshaped Americans' understanding of other peoples and cultures, is the subject of this book.

What I examine here are the ways in which America's first international companies positioned their actions — selling commodities overseas to increase revenues — as part of the civilizing process (that is, as a way of sharing the benefits of industrial development with others) and how, in turn, this positioning created different meanings of and knowledges about other peoples, nations, cultures, and places. I focus on the cultures of business, using businessmen and women (managers, advertisers, corporate presidents, salesmen) as the "cultural mediators" whose images and texts were constituted from, and in turn contributed to, one of the major narratives of American expansionism. The story of American expansionism, as the first quote at the beginning of this chapter suggests, starts with the notion of American exceptionalism based on a moral and political superiority over Europe. However, these commercial "cultural mediators" add to this story in two ways: first, they imply that American superiority is a fact that is reflected in and can be judged by the quality and quantity of its manufactures, not in its colonial conquests; second, they add a dynamic and fluid quality to this equation of commodities and morality, such that industrial commodities are seen to lead to "peace" in other *places* over *time*.

This is a book, then, about the United States and its business cultures; it does not directly address the impact of American goods on, and the narratives they brought with them to, other places. I interpret the cultural representations produced by five of the largest American international companies in the late 19th and early 20th centuries — Singer Manufacturing Company[3] (and its various subsidiaries), McCormick Harvesting Machine Company (International Harvester after 1902), H.J. Heinz Company, Eastman Kodak Company, and the New York Life Insurance Company (though I focus on the first three) — in relationship to the particular international experiences and cultures of these companies and the larger socioeconomic context and ideological formations of turn-of-the-century America. By so doing, I add another, and at times different, layer to our understanding of imperialism — that is, to our understanding of how power is imposed on people and places beyond national borders. The companies I examine produced visual and verbal images of foreign worlds and cultures that made the purchase of American commodities by foreigners appear normal and inevitable, and thus made it seem only natural that the United States would continue to supply the world with its industrial products. Foreign peoples and nations, in other words, were positioned as consumers, as feminized subjects, with the United States positioned as the masculine producer. In this way, the contested and complex story of American economic dominance over large portions of the world came to be seen by many Americans as inevitable and as natural as the patriarchal family. This was accomplished through a reiteration of a particular set of visual and verbal stories about "others" living outside the borders of the United States, stories that emphasized access to commodities as a way of signaling difference, reinforcing contemporary racial thinking that associated whiteness with industrial development.[4] Yet the focus on commodities opened the possibility that "others" could in fact become white, with all the attendant anxieties that such a "shock of sameness"[5] might produce. As a result, the stories these early American international companies told about "others" were comprised of various strategies to reassert difference, strategies that were often contradictory but nonetheless remained rooted to the expansion of consumption.

This understanding is important to the ongoing critical reassessment of imperialism — what has been called a critical postcolonial perspective — that has been undertaken by geographers, historians, cultural theorists, and others. American imperialism has, until recently, been understood in terms of its territorial and political claims, commencing with the Spanish-American War and continuing with increasing vigor through to the late 20th century as the United States became the dominant global power.[6] In this view, the story of American imperialism is a narrative dominated by the movement of troops, capital, and resources. It is about conquest, production, and destruction. Yet, as scholars are now showing, a complementary but different story of imperialism also needs to be told, one that is as much about "civilization" and consumption as it is about conquest and production.[7] This form of imperialism was perhaps more subtle than what scholars have examined, but it was no less effective in creating systems of global economic and political dominance. In fact, one could argue that a primary instrument for the spread of American influence in the late 19th and 20th centuries has been the selling of consumer products. It is no coincidence that the so-called "American Century"[8] is also what Gary Cross calls "an all-consuming century"[9]; in other words, the United States' ascendancy throughout the 20th century into a position of global dominance coincides with, and in fact I will argue is inseparable from, the dominance of an American-style consumer culture and economy over national and international spaces.

For much of the 19th and 20th centuries, American foreign and economic policy was geared not toward the establishment of formal colonies but toward the expansion of markets. For the most part, the United States' political and economic elites were not interested in establishing territorial colonies, nor did they want to be involved in the administration of political subjects. Rather, they sought worldwide markets for American mass-produced goods.[10] Why they chose to do so — in other words, why the United States embarked on economic instead of territorial expansion — is a question scholars have long pondered and one that requires close attention to the particular historical and geographical contexts in which American economy, society, and culture were formed.[11] The focus on mass production and consumption can be partially explained by the relatively high cost of labor in the United States (leading to the development of a type of capitalism that was reliant on profitability through high levels of productivity and that fostered technological innovations); by the push to take advantage of economies of scale within the expanding and seemingly endless markets of the "frontier"; and by a culture that early on required material acquisition as the determinant of status or class. With an overriding political ethos that favored individual rights as the "key" to democracy, and without the immediate need to engage in European power struggles, the United States' economic and political elites simply followed a path to economic growth that was well honed from their experiences creating a national market; empire-making in the sense of colonial acquisitions was beside the point. The United States was engaged primarily in informal imperialism, in promoting trade and economic integration that suited the needs of American corporations. American empire, then, was as much about ordinary commercial transactions as it was about political maneuvers or military interventions. Imperialism in this sense was enacted daily — on the docks, in the grocery stores, and at home. Decades before the Spanish-American War, American businesses were developing international marketing strategies, establishing shipping and transport networks, and reaping the rewards of an expanded consumer market. At first, in the 1870s and 1880s, the primary markets for American goods were the countries comprising Western and Eastern Europe (including Russia) and Canada. Later, depending on the particular commodity, other important markets included Mexico, Argentina, Brazil, India, Japan, Turkey, Thailand, China, South Africa, Chile, and Peru.

This is not to deny, however, that the United States also engaged in formal imperialism, sending large armies into Mexico in 1846 and establishing what can only be called "colonies" in Cuba, Guam, Hawaii, the Philippines, and Puerto Rico through military and political manipulations coincident with the 1898 Spanish-American War. The causal relationships between America's formal and informal imperialism are complex, to say the least, and not always as one would expect. For example, although most American international companies supported the 1898 war for patriotic reasons (it was an incredibly popular war), many of the major players in America's boardrooms did not favor any future military incursions, finding that wars and imperial governance got in the way of trade and marketing.[12] On the other hand, America's formal imperialism, particularly in the Philippines, did lead to increased trade and economic integration, but this economic activity was basically inconsequential when compared to America's primary markets in such places as Russia, Argentina, and Brazil. Compared to the importance of economic integration within the British formal imperial world, United States' formal empire contributed relatively little to the global reach of American companies.[13]

That American goods competed successfully even with British-made products attests to the formidable strength of American mass production technologies and to the innovative marketing strategies pursued by many entrepreneurs.[14] In other words, America's economic imperialism was based primarily on the making and selling of mass-produced commodities. Scientific innovation combined with Taylorist production facilities allowed American manufacturers to produce "modern," affordable commodities — at least to middle-class families. Fairly well-connected rail and shipping networks developed throughout the latter half of the 19th century, made it possible to move these goods over large distances, both within the United States and outside its borders. New marketing and advertising strategies, such as the establishment of overseas retail outlets, literally put the names of American-produced commodities on the streets and in the homes of people from London to Peking to Buenos Aires. And as U.S. companies capitalized on their competitive advantages in the mass production of commodities to effectively export and market their products overseas, the U.S. government pursued a foreign policy that enabled these endeavors.[15]

As a result, in distinction to the type of imperialism generally recognized by geographers and political scientists, the United States' extension of power beyond its national borders proceeded through other channels, created multiple meanings and knowledges, and fashioned different types of geopolitical and spatial arrangements. In this primarily economic empire, the "others" that Americans were confronting were considered not political subjects but potential consumers, and worldviews were derived as much from a logic of profit and loss as they were from an outlook based on a racialized "family tree of man."[16] In other words, what I argue in this book is that America's companies produced a narrative of progress — a temporally fluid view of culture and place — within which all people were potential consumers and all nations potentially modern.

Until relatively recently, very little has been written about the cultural implications of American commercial imperialism. The messy and interconnected histories and geographies of colonial and commercial expansion have often been simplified through recourse to the binary "economy/culture," with "economy" being the primary lens through which commercial expansion has been viewed, and "culture" serving that purpose for colonial rule. Yet case studies detailing the imposition of power over peoples and spaces that we call "imperialism" have alerted us to the inseparability of economic and cultural claims to power; in other words, to study one of these aspects of imperial rule necessarily involves examining the other. On the one hand, as Gordon Stewart[17] has shown, even within the context of a "down-to-earth" activity such as jute manufacturing in colonial India, the cultural discourse of civilization was at play. "Imperialism," he concludes, "was much more than the product of its economic aspects."[18] On the other, that same discourse of civilization that was so fundamental to Americans' ordering of space and time and relationships with "others" was, according to Matthew Frye Jacobson, "at its core ... an economic concept."[19] As Jacobson elaborates, production, sales, and profits were as fundamental to the late 19th and early 20th centuries' verbal and visual language of difference as were morality, religion, and civilization.

Much of this scholarly recognition of the inseparability of the economic and cultural aspects of imperialism stems from studies of the commodity cultures of empire within the context of late 19th and early 20th century Britain — studies that range from analyses of World's Exhibitions, department store displays, popular music, clothing styles, and advertising strategies.[20] This series of works has established how colonial pursuits reshaped imaginations, identities, and everyday practices through the emerging culture of mass commodification within turn-of-the-century Great Britain. Other studies have examined similar effects of imperial commodity culture within the colonial world. Timothy Burke's fascinating historical analysis of the marketing of hygienic products in Zimbabwe shows how selling products beyond national borders often meant reshaping people's identities and cultures — in this case, how selling manufactured soap meant convincing people of the efficacy of Western notions of personal and social hygiene and establishing Western ideals of bodily beauty.[21] Similarly, the essays in David Howes' edited collection *Cross-Cultural Consumption* focus on the trade of consumer products produced within one cultural context and sold to another, providing empirical studies of the cultural malleability of commodities — in other words, of how the same product can change meaning given its particular cultural context.[22]

Each of these studies adds different inflections to our understanding of how colonialism coincided with commodity capitalism, and each has done so with explicit attention to culture. Shifting that analysis to the case of the United States means shifting the frame of reference away from colonialism per se, and more toward a recognition of different forms of empire. In fact, given that the U.S. overseas expansion occurred primarily without direct government intervention, it might be difficult to describe the process as imperial. In the cases I examine here, corporate presidents, advertising executives, and salesmen and saleswomen were the primary agents for the exertion of American power, and that power was enacted not through laws but through everyday acts of desiring and consuming. Part of the analysis in this book, then, points to the various limits of using an imperial framework for understanding American economic expansion overseas.

Yet recent work within critical geopolitics has begun to explore the ways in which it is important to think of America as an empire, providing historical background and analysis for understanding contemporary American imperial claims.[23] This work focuses, for the most part, on the economic and political processes and ramifications of American expansionism, with little attention paid to such "cultural" matters as gender, race, identity, and performance. On the other hand, works that have examined such cultural matters have for the most part limited their geographical and temporal scales of reference to those times and places when the United States undertook what could be called "formal" imperial actions[24] — that is, territorial and political claims to power over peoples outside the United States (such as in the Philippines, Hawaii, Cuba, Guam, Puerto Rico, and Mexico in the 19th century and Panama, Vietnam, Nicaragua, and Iraq in the 20th and 21st centuries). However, if we expand this analysis to include Mark Crinson's notion of informal imperialism,[25] then studies of the relationships between cultural and economic imperialism within the context of the United States can move beyond these parameters. In this book, I show the various ways that an American informal empire, held together by economic transactions, functioned culturally in the late 19th and early 20th centuries. To do so, I borrow insights gained from similar analyses within the context of the British colonial empire, asking all along in what ways it matters (or not) that an American empire operated not primarily through territorial but through economic claims to power. I analyze the particular discursive and material ways that American products were sold in parts of the world where commodities, not armies or politicians, did the work of colonization.

To do so requires attention to the specificities of each company's internal practices and cultural products as well as to the socioeconomic, political, and ideological context of the United States during the last decades of the 19th century and the first decades of the 20th century. In the following chapters, then, I pay attention to both the particularities of the companies and their corporate cultures and to the ideological and socioeconomic context in which these cultures developed. Chapter 1 lays some of the groundwork for this study by examining the geographical and economic extent of America's informal empire and the sociospatial practices that enabled it to function.

Based on my case studies, I argue that that the sociospatial practices that created these overseas commercial empires were surprisingly little different from the practices that created similar spaces at home — the guiding principles of economic geography reigned supreme in both. I also suggest that unlike material expressions of formal empire, such as government buildings, elite housing complexes, and redesigned urban plans, these spaces of informal economic empire were far less imposing and far more banal. I then turn to the various representations these companies produced — their images of race, culture, gender, and ethnicity that formed narratives of progress. I do so by focusing on the particular corporate cultures and advertising strategies of Singer, Heinz, and McCormick/International Harvester. Singer Manufacturing Company, I show, created stories about other peoples in the world that presented them as essentially similar to Americans, all potentially able to become "white" through proper consumption. This erasure of difference, however, was enabled by a reassertion of geographical difference — that is, by showing in both image and word that these "others" lived in areas geographically distant from the United States. Through its yearly illustrated catalogs, McCormick/International Harvester presented similar types of stories about the world, focusing on how machinery and technology could make countries and cultures modern and American, although always reaffirming geographical difference. With its paternal corporate culture, H.J. Heinz Company created a view of other peoples as part of an extended family and of economic activity overseas as an extension of world travel. Taken together, these three case studies, I suggest, produced narratives that, on one hand, emphasized the fluidity of foreign cultures as they moved toward modernity yet, on the other hand, reasserted the importance of geographical boundaries to keep people in their proper place. Instead of the geographically mobile stories that often accompany contemporary global narratives, these early international companies created images of fixed regional and national boundaries.

I conclude by tracing the ideological linkages between these late 19th- and early 20th-century corporate "stories" about the world and two related but different sets of geographical "stories" — the new "scientific" commercial geographies that were being published in the first half of the 20th century, and the policy statements that constituted the post-World War II discourses of economic development. The new commercial geography textbooks and knowledges that were circulating in the first half of the 20th century gave scientific legitimacy to a way of seeing other peoples and cultures that was already familiar to many Americans through the stories told them by commodities and their advertising. With scientific legitimacy, this set of ideas — what I call *flexible racism* — that was already circulating widely in the United States formed one of the key strands of thought integral to the discourses of economic development. In other words, I conclude the book by showing the ways in which these corporate "metanarratives" of U.S. expansionism both complicate and anticipate other forms of "metanarratives" that have circulated in the so-called American century. The stories of universality through commerce that these early American international companies created in the last decades of the 19th century were important antecedents to the more scientific and political stories of economic development that followed.

To start, let me briefly outline the historical contours of late Victorian America, particularly its ideological components, in order to provide adequate context for understanding my analysis of the commercial stories that follow in the next several chapters.

Civilization and Consumption in Turn-of-the-Century America

I center my study on the last quarter of the 19th century and the first decade of the 20th century, a time that witnessed the first efflorescence of consumer culture in the United States and that was ideologically dominated by the discourse of civilization. It is within this context that the first American companies began to seek international markets. What I show in this book is the ways in which this "corporate internationalism" shaped how Americans began to view other peoples and places and their own role within the world. Certainly the changes within the United States during this time period were vast. In 1876, the Centennial Exhibition held in Philadelphia to commemorate the 100th anniversary of American independence expressed the coming of age of the United States — its maturation to "manhood" through the turbulence and trials of nation-building, western expansion, industrialization, and the Civil War. The 1893 Columbian Exposition held in Chicago to celebrate the 400th anniversary of Columbus's "discovery" of America was meant to express the cultural superiority and sophistication of American life and its new place on the world's stage. And the 1915 Panama-Pacific International Exposition, a celebration of the opening of the Panama Canal, marked the arrival of the United States as the dominant economic power in the world.

In the 39 years that separated these three expositions, the United States had witnessed significant changes. In 1876, the U.S. military was still in the process of conquering and sequestering native populations;

in 1893, Frederick Jackson Turner announced that America had seen the last of its internal frontier, setting the stage for the opening of different frontiers in Cuba, the Philippines, and elsewhere. By 1893, the country could boast of industrial and financial superiority over England, of a successful negotiation through reconstruction after the Civil War, and of the fulfillment of its "manifest destiny" — Anglo settlement from the Atlantic to the Pacific.[26] Its industries had entered a new phase of mass production for a national and, increasingly, international audience.[27] Now that the country had completed its territorial expansion, production stepped up to meet the large-scale and spatially diverse demands. By 1915, American industries dominated most aspects of world trade — international sales, production, and financial activities — leading to what we could call today the globalization of industrial development.[28] Many American companies had established manufacturing sites in locations suited to labor and resource demands, disregarding political borders, and had developed extensive international sales and financial networks.

Part and parcel of this economic dominance was corporate attention to the importance of advertising and promotion. The expositions themselves were filled with corporate advertisements, highlighting what had become an increasing part of Americans' everyday life — consumer activities and advertising.[29] Trade cards, followed by advertising in national magazines, brought images of corporate identity into the homes of most middle-class Americans.[30] Many of these new national and international companies drew on images of American identity to sell their products, aligning American "civilization" with a white, Anglo, middle-class, patriarchal family. In other words, these companies drew on the complex discourse of civilization and gave that discourse a particular American spin.[31]

As an ideology that orders both time and space along a rigid hierarchy, the complex nexus of ideas encompassed in the binary civilization/savagery can be traced throughout Western history, dating at least to the ancient Greeks, who posited reason as the distinguishing mark of civilized humanity. As Kay Anderson argues, its elaboration and entwinement with Darwinian theories of evolution in the 19th century applied the distinction between human/animal to that between different peoples or "races": "If to be 'human' was to hold the capacity for ascent out of instinct/savagery, then, the superiority of some humans over others could be made to stand analogously to the superiority of primitive peoples over apes."[32]

By the late 19th century, this ideology that "naturalized" the "superiority of some humans over others" dominated the discourse of imperialism. Within this discourse, human history was envisioned as an evolutionary process that began in a remote past as a stage of savagery and that moved inexorably and inevitably through various stages of barbarism to reach civilization. Only the white race, though, had fully evolved and reached the stage of civilization. As Gail Bederman has observed, in this sense, "civilization" was akin to a racial trait, inherited only by the "advanced" and superior white races.[33] The "races" of the world, therefore, could be sorted out by evolutionary stage and stratified hierarchically, with the savage races on the bottom and the civilized ones at the top. If human history progressed through racialized stages, human geography was similarly racialized; some portions of the world were inhabited by inferior, savage races, others by barbaric races (violent and warlike), and others (portions of Europe and the United States) by superior, civilized white races.

Gender figured into this equation in two ways. First, adherence to Victorian gender roles was seen as indicative of civilization. In other words, in a fully civilized society, women's and men's roles diverged but were complementary. Civilized women were passive and delicate; they were the family's caretakers and the keepers of society's morals and sentiments. Civilized men were manly — that is, they were self-controlled, rational and were the providers of the economic and physical well-being of women and children. In savage societies, women were seen as coarse, often performing manual labor similar to men, whereas men were irrational, given to emotional outbursts and unburdened with the responsibilities of providing for women and children. In Bederman's words, "in short, the pronounced sexual differences celebrated in the middle class's doctrine of separate spheres were assumed to be absent in savagery, but to be an intrinsic and necessary aspect of higher civilization."[34] Societies characterized by manly men and delicate women indicated the highest evolutionary stage of humankind.

Gender was important in another way; if women were seen as the caretakers of civilized society's morals and sentiments, they could in some sense be seen as the active agents of civilization. In other words, part of the proper Victorian women's role (and therefore of the civilized woman) was to maintain society's Christian ideals and instill those values into their children, thereby ensuring and perpetuating the continuation of civilization. Somewhat paradoxically (in the sense that passivity, not activity, characterized Victorian women's prescribed roles), women were seen as the civilizers of society — that is, as active agents in the production of civilization.

This social maintenance becomes particularly interesting when we consider that part of what fueled late 19th century Western society was its commitment to what Bederman calls a "Darwinist version of

Protestant millennialism."[35] The popularization of Darwin's theories of evolution in the latter part of the 19th century put a particular spin on what had been a long-held belief in American Christian culture: that human history had only one "cosmic purpose," which was to crusade against evil, and each successful battle brought humankind closer to the millennium when Christ would rule over a righteous world. Discourses of civilization provided a way of reconciling evolutionary theory with this teleological belief in the movement of human history toward some type of perfection: instead of a deity working to move humans toward perfection, evolution could do the trick. Good against evil was refigured as superior civilized races "outsurviving"[36] inferior races. And all good Christians had as their duty to work toward this perfect society, a society of perfect "womanliness" and "manliness." As Bederman observes, "this millennial vision of perfected racial evolution and gender specialization was what people meant when they referred to 'the advancement of civilization.'"[37] Civilizing savage "races" helped pave the road to this perfect society. And because women were viewed as integral to this civilizing process, it was of the utmost importance that their feminine roles be maintained. If civilization itself was defined by adherence to appropriate gender roles, civilized societies had to be populated by manly men and womanly women, and part of what defined a womanly woman was her role as a civilizer and domesticator of society.

Although this discourse of civilization/savagery has deep roots within Judeo-Christian culture and a complex history, its particular formulation in the late 19th century was intricately connected to commodity capitalism.[38] Western products were seen as active agents in the "civilizing" process and proof that one had achieved the stage of "civilization." Correct consumption, then, was not simply a social necessity but was a national imperative. For those living distant from the core areas of American power, and for those new to the United States, purchasing American products became akin to participating in American "civilization." "Consumption," in the words of Stuart Ewen, "assumed an ideological veil of nationalism and democratic lingo."[39] And American companies, particularly those that were international, were quick to adopt and adapt this "ideological veil" to fit their advertising needs, using their international experiences to align their products with civilizing experience and using the discourse of civilization to legitimize their international sales. This book, therefore, focuses on how the discourse of civilization — this complex, often contradictory, and powerful set of ideas — both supported and was itself strengthened by the visual and verbal languages used to market American products overseas and at home.[40] Yet, before I turn to my in-depth analyses of these corporate "civilizing" stories, I set the stage, as it were, by outlining their material bases — the spatial expanse and sociospatial processes that constituted an American commercial empire in the late 19th and early 20th centuries.

Endnotes

1. Walter LaFeber's analysis that traces lines of continuity between the emergence and development of America's industrial system and the Spanish-American War remains a convincing argument for looking to the mid-19th century to understand American imperialism. See LaFeber's *The New Empire: An Interpretation of American Expansion, 1860–1898* (Ithaca, NY: Cornell University Press, 1998). Yet those historical linkages are often overlooked by scholars more focused on examining contemporary American imperialism. See, for example, the essays in Anne Godlewska and Neil Smith, eds., *Geography and Empire* (Cambridge, MA: Blackwell, 1994) and Amy Kaplan and Donald E. Pease, eds., *Cultures of United States Imperialism* (Durham, NC: Duke University Press, 1993).

2. Mark Crinson, *Empire Building: Orientalism and Victorian Architecture* (New York: Routledge, 1996:2). For a more detailed discussion of the various meanings of informal empire, see Robin W. Winks, "On Decolonization and Informal Empire," *American Historical Review*, 81, 1976: 540–556.

3. The Singer Manufacturing Company was incorporated under this name in 1863, and remained as such throughout much of the period I discuss in this book. Today, the company is called Singer Sewing Company. I've chosen to refer to the company under its late 19th and early 20th century name.

4. Racialized thinking no doubt undergirded the stories of consumption that I discuss throughout this book. My emphasis here is on understanding the connections, and potential contradictions, between contemporary racial ideologies and the demands of capital to expand beyond U.S. borders. For key works that examine relationships between racial formations and U.S. imperialism, see Eric T.L. Love, *Race Over Empire: Racism and U.S. Imperialism, 1865–1900* (Chapel Hill, NC: University of North Carolina Press, 2004); Gail Bederman, *Manliness and Civilization: A Cultural History of Gender and Race in the United States, 1880–1917* (Chicago: University of Chicago Press, 1995); Laura Wexler, *Tender Violence: Domestic Visions in an Age of U.S. Imperialism* (Chapel Hill, NC: University of North Carolina Press, 2000); Rubin F. Weston, *Racism in U.S. Imperialism: The Influence of Racial Assumptions on American Foreign Policy, 1893–1946* (Columbia, SC: University of South Carolina Press, 1972); and Paul A. Kramer, "Empires, Exceptions, and Anglo-Saxons: Race and Rule between the British and United States

Empires, 1880–1910," *Journal of American History,* 88 (4), 2002: 1315–53.

5. Bobby M. Wilson, "Race in Commodity Exchange and Consumption: Separate but Equal," *Annals of the Association of American Geographers,* 95 (3), 2005: 595.

6. See, for example, Kaplan and Pease (1993); Walter A. McDougall, *Promised Land, Crusader State: The American Encounter with the World since 1776* (Boston: Houghton Mifflin, 1997); and Godlewska and Smith (1994).

7. Matthew Frye Jacobson, *Barbarian Virtues: The United States Encounters Foreign Peoples at Home and Abroad, 1876–1917* (New York: Hill and Wang, 2000); Lori Merish, *Sentimental Materialism: Gender, Commodity Culture, and Nineteenth-Century American Literature* (Durham, NC: Duke University Press, 2000); Wexler (2000); Ann Stoler, "Tense and Tender Ties: The Politics of Comparison in North American History and (Post)Colonial Studies," *Journal of American History,* 88, 2001: 829–65; and Michael Adas, "From Settler Colony to Global Hegemon: Integrating the Exceptionalist Narrative of the American Experience into World History," *American Historical Review,* 106, 2001: 1692–1720.

8. Henry R. Luce, *The American Century* (New York: Farrar and Rinehart, 1941); David Slater and Peter Taylor, eds., *The American Century: Consensus and Coercion in the Projection of American Power* (Malden, MA: Blackwell Publishers, 1999).

9. Gary Cross, *An All-Consuming Century: Why Commercialism Won in Modern America* (New York: Columbia University Press, 2000).

10. For more detailed accounts of the significance of economic expansion in late 19th and early 20th century America, see LaFeber (1998), Mira Wilkins, *The Emergence of Multinational Enterprise: American Business Abroad from the Colonial Era to 1914* (Cambridge, MA: Harvard University Press, 1970); Emily S. Rosenberg, *Spreading the American Dream: American Economic and Cultural Expansion, 1890–1945* (New York: Hill and Wang, 1982); Emily S. Rosenberg, *Financial Missionaries to the World: The Politics and Culture of Dollar Diplomacy, 1900–1930* (Durham, NC: Duke Universiry Press, 2003).

11. John A. Agnew has provided the most compelling and historically rich account of the distinctive shape of American "empire." See his *Hegemony: The New Shape of Global Power* (Philadelphia: Temple University Press, 2005), particularly chapter 4, and his introductory chapter in *American Space/American Place: Geographies of the Contemporary United States* (New York: Routledge, 2002), edited by John A. Agnew and Jonathan M. Smith. For more detailed accounts of the particular form of capitalism that took shape in the 19th and early 20th centuries in the United States, see Meghnad Desai, *Marx's Revenge: The Resurgence of Capitalism and the Death of*

Statist Socialism (New York: Verso, 2002) and Mike Davis, *Prisoners of the American Dream: Politics and Economy in the History of the U.S. Working Class* (London: Verso, 1986).

12. The corporate archives of Singer, McCormick, and the New York Life Insurance Company are littered with references to the disruptions of wars and the loss to business that they cause. In Russia, for example (one of the primary markets for Singer and McCormick), agents and salesmen were directed to continue their work as best they could throughout the Russian-Japanese War of 1904 to 1905.

13. Stephen Constantine, *The Making of British Colonial Development Policy, 1914–1940* (Totowa, NJ: Frank Cass and Company, 1984); Stephen Constantine, "'Bringing the Empire Alive': The Empire Marketing Board and Imperial Propaganda, 1926–1933," in *Imperialism and Popular Culture* John M. Mackenzie, ed., (Dover, NH: Manchester University Press, 1986), 192–231; and Stephen Constantine, "Anglo-Canadian Relations, the Empire Marketing Board and Canadian Autonomy between the Wars," *Journal of Imperial and Commonwealth History*, 21 (1993): 357–84.

14. Rosenberg (1982).

15. LaFeber (1998).

16. Anne McClintock, *Imperial Leather: Race, Gender, and Sexuality in the Colonial Contest* (New York: Routledge, 1995), 39.

17. Gordon T. Stewart, *Jute and Empire: The Calcutta Jute Wallahs and the Landscapes of Empire* (Manchester, UK: Manchester University Press, 1998).

18. Stewart (1998), 233.

19. Jacobson (2000), 50.

20. See, for example, Jeffrey A. Auerbach, *The Great Exhibition of 1851: A Nation on Display* (New Haven, CT: Yale University Press, 1999); Paul Greenhalgh, *Ephemeral Vistas: The Expositions Universelles, Great Exhibitions and World's Fairs, 1851–1939* (Manchester, UK: Manchester University Press, 1988); Mica Nava, "The Cosmopolitanism of Commerce and the Allure of Difference: Selfridges, the Russian Ballet and the Tango 1911–1914," *International Journal of Cultural Studies*, 1 (1998): 163–196; Penny Summerfield, "Patriotism and Empire: Music-Hall Entertainment," in Mackenzie (1986), 17–48; Christopher Breward, "Sartorial Spectacle: Clothing and Masculine Identities in the Imperial City, 1860–1914," in *Imperial Cities: Landscape, Display, and Identity* Felix Driver and David Gilbert, (Manchester, UK: Manchester University Press, 1999), 238–53; McClintock (1995); Thomas Richards, *The Commodity Culture of Victorian England: Advertising and Spectacle, 1851–1914* (Stanford, CA: Stanford University Press, 1990).

21. Timothy Burke, *Lifebuoy Men, Lux Women: Commodification, Consumption, and Cleanliness in Modern Zimbabwe* (Durham, NC: Duke University Press, 1996).

22. David Howes, ed., *Cross-Cultural Consumption: Global Markets, Local Realities* (New York: Routledge, 1996).

23. See, for example, Neil Smith, *American Empire: Roosevelt's Geographer and the Prelude to Globalization* (Berkeley, CA: University of California Press, 2003) and John A. Agnew and Joanne Sharp, "America, Frontier Nation: From Abstract Space to Worldly Place," in Agnew and Smith (2002), 79–107.

24. See, for example, the essays in Kaplan and Pease (1993) and Wexler (2000). The essays in Gilbert M. Joseph, Catherine C. LeGrand, and Ricardo D. Salvatore, eds., *Close Encounters of Empire: Writing the Cultural History of U.S.-Latin American Relations* (Durham, NC: Duke University Press, 1998) provide cultural readings of the informal power of the United States, limited though to the countries of Latin America.

25. Crinson (1996).

26. Gertjan Dijkink, *National Identity and Geopolitical Visions: Maps of Pride and Pain* (New York: Routledge, 1996).

27. Susan Strasser, *Satisfaction Guaranteed: The Making of the American Mass Market* (New York: Pantheon Books, 1989); Rosenberg (1982).

28. Wilkins (1970).

29. William Leach, *Land of Desire: Merchants, Power, and the Rise of a New American Culture* (New York: Pantheon Books, 1993); Jackson Lears, *Fables of Abundance: A Cultural History of Advertising in America* (New York: Basic Books, 1994).

30. Ellen Gruber Garvey, *The Adman in the Parlor: Magazines and the Gendering of Consumer Culture, 1880s to 1910s* (New York: Oxford University Press, 1996).

31. The most incisive analyses of civilization versus savagery as an ideological framework for 19th century imperialism can be found in Bederman (1995); Louise Michele Newman, *White Women's Rights: The Racial Origins of Feminism in the United States* (New York: Oxford University Press, 1999); and McClintock (1995).

32. K. Anderson, "'The Beast Within': Race, Humanity, and Animality," *Environment and Planning D: Society and Space* 18 (2000): 301–320.

33. Bederman (1995), 25.

34. Ibid.

35. Ibid.

36. Ibid., 26.

37. Ibid.

38. Bederman (1995); Newman (1999); Jacobson (2000).

39. Stuart Ewen, *Captains of Consciousness: Advertising and the Social Roots of the Consumer Culture* (New York: McGraw-Hill Book Company, 1976), 42.

40. My point here is that the ideas encapsulated under the rubric of "civilization" were protean and elastic enough to legitimize both cultural "missionary" efforts — literally, the efforts to elevate the world to a level of American "whiteness" — and those efforts that were primarily about selling more products. In fact, the apparent separation of the two is anachronistic, a result of late 20th century thinking that posits clear divisions between economy and culture.

2

The Geographies
of Commercial Empire

After 28 years of doing business in Russia through its own agents
and those of its predecessors, my Company feels that we should further establish ourselves as Russian by manufacture of our machines
in Russia. We already have branch offices for managing the sale of
our machines at Odessa, Charkow, Rostow, Riga, Moscow, Samara,
Omsk and Vladivostok.
— C.H. McCormick, July 5, 1909, St. Petersburg, transcription of interview
between McCormick; Montgomery Schuyler, First Secretary of the United
States Embassy; and Mr. Krivochein, Russian Minister of Agriculture.

When there last year I noticed several points in the business which
seemed to demand immediate attention, and wrote you 8th July
1890 to discuss them. The principal decisions then arrived at were
to suppress the 15% Cash Discount, and to introduce the modern
canvassing ideas so far as they could be applied to such a peculiar
Country.
— Audit of Switzerland Office, September 1891, by G.B. Dobson, Singer
archives

America's informal empire was a material as much as an ideological
configuration. As the above quotes make clear, creating and maintaining a commercial empire required extensive and intensive material investments and complex negotiations. When Cyrus McCormick,
speaking on behalf of the newly formed International Harvester (IH)
Corporation, finalized plans to construct a major manufacturing

plant outside of Moscow in 1909, he was following a principle of economic geography — with high transport costs, it made economic sense for IH to locate a plant to manufacture its agricultural implements close to its fast-growing market in Russia. Singer Manufacturing Company also began to invest in overseas manufacturing in the late 19th century to help supply the demand for machines created by its spatially extensive and capital intensive sales and distribution networks. As the second quote above suggests, Singer managers visited foreign offices, assessed sales, and implemented changes to increase profits on a regular basis throughout its international network, quite a laborious and expensive monitoring procedure.

As early 1876, some American companies were already building trade networks and retail shops throughout much of Europe and Central and South America. By 1915, that empire had become much more extensive in its spatial reach and intensive, both in terms of the amount of business it represented for American companies and in terms of its real estate investments. In addition to retail shops and sales agencies, American companies built and managed manufacturing plants, resource extraction sites, and headquarter and other office buildings. This sort of extensive commercial empire was first made possible by the incredible investments in transportation technologies. Although hardly reaching the scale of contemporary global networking, the international shipping and rail networks that allowed for the commercial expansion of the United States in the late 19th and early 20th centuries were fairly well developed, and by the standards of their time, quite vast. Between 1870 and 1910, railway mileage in the United States expanded almost fivefold (from 52,922 to 249,902), with a similar rate of increase in Russia (7,098 to 34,990) and an even greater rate of expansion in India (4,771 to 32,099).[1] A series of technological innovations in steamship design and refrigeration made possible the massive expansion of transoceanic shipping, including the transport of chilled meat by the 1880s. The major result of these innovations and establishment of new routes was a drastic decline in transport costs. Estimates suggest that costs on the Atlantic trade routes declined an average of 1.5% per year between 1870 and 1910.[2] American companies capitalized on these innovations and cost-savings, establishing regular shipping routes and transportation networks that allowed their mass-produced goods and services to reach their potential markets.

Yet to take full advantage of these shared infrastructural developments, American companies required their own investments in space and place. For companies that were primarily interested in selling commodities, commercial expansion required investments in the exchange of goods (importing and exporting businesses, wholesalers); selling of goods (establishing ties to foreign retail agencies, constructing company-owned shops); and maintenance of goods and capital (buildings and offices to house managers, accountants, clerks). Other considerations were required for foreign manufacture, including research into and attention paid to the location of raw materials, the location and design of production sites, and supplies and costs of labor.

The American economic empire, in other words, was marked with and constituted through complex business transactions and relationships. Yet "doing business" in and with other countries required a more flexible view of world order than what has generally been called "colonial" — a view in which nations are fixed as either colonizers or colonies. In the more commercial worldview that characterized American international companies, foreign nations as potential consumers were considered similar in kind, if not in fact, to each other and to the United States, with no clear delineation between colony and colonizer.[3] American companies learned to accommodate the particular demands and needs of foreign nations and peoples by altering their business plans and strategies, incorporating what was useful and profitable. In this way, they created consumers out of foreigners.

Drawing on the cases of Singer, McCormick (IH), Heinz, Kodak, and New York Life Insurance (NYLIC), I first provide an overview of the spatial expansion of American companies overseas in the late 19th and early 20th centuries, before turning to in-depth case studies of the processes involved in this expansion: the establishment of and practices involved in Singer's elaborate marketing networks in Russia and India, and the decision-making process that lay behind McCormick's decision to build its first overseas manufacturing plants in Sweden, Russia, Germany, and France. What becomes clear through these examinations is the various ways that these American companies tried to impose their habits of doing business on foreign nations and peoples, while at the same time being forced to recognize, accommodate, and adapt to "foreign" customs and peoples.

Constructing the Commercial Empire: 1860-1889

The American Civil War was an important turning point for many American manufacturing companies, such as the relatively new Singer Manufacturing Company (begun in 1851).[4] To compensate for the lowered internal demand for products, caused by the disruptions of war, particularly the loss of sales in the American south, Edward Clark, the company's president, began the push for overseas sales. Experimenting first in France, the company soon realized that the standard methods of foreign sales — selling through a foreign agent or commission house (who often sold more than one brand of sewing machine) were unreliable and nonlucrative. As a result, Clark decided to develop a sales system overseas similar to its internal one, that is, the establishment of branch offices controlled by Singer Company, each of which employed its own sales force. This certainly was a capital-intensive scheme, but based on its success with the American market, Singer moved quickly to build this system overseas. By the mid-1860s, Singer was selling its machines, either through direct sales via retail shops that they had established or through contract agreements with other retailers, in Canada, Mexico, Russia, Scotland, England, Spain, France, Germany, Sweden, Puerto Rico, Cuba, Curaçao, Venezuela, Uruguay, and Peru.[5] By the end of the Civil War, Singer's foreign sales accounted for more than 40% of its total sales, and by 1879, foreign sales outnumbered domestic sales.[6] (See Figure 2.1.)

At this point, with Singer's New Jersey plant unable to produce enough machines to meet demand, Clark decided to initiate manufacturing overseas and began construction of a plant outside of Glasgow, which soon expanded to the town of Kilbowie and was completed in 1885. This facility could produce 10,000 machines per week, keeping up with the new demand created throughout Europe. George McKenzie, who became president in 1882, moved forward aggressively in other foreign markets, trying to counter tariffs and other tax issues that were working against sales in Europe. He was particularly keen on increasing sales in Asia, given what the company assessed as its vast size and underdeveloped nature. Singer executives also considered Asia to be untouched by the economic downturns of 1882 and 1883 that injured markets throughout the United States and Europe. When China proved very disappointing for sales, Singer turned its attention to Japan, where sales seemed more promising. By 1889, when the company's new president, Frederick Bourne, took charge, Singer was a fully multinational company, with "foreign manufacturing and sales" representing the "bulk of the company's assets and revenues."[7]

Singer was the only company whose international business dominated their accounting sheets in 1889, but other types of businesses were beginning to move to this level of internationalization. NYLIC, for example, had begun to sell policies overseas as early as 1870; by 1889, those policies totaled roughly one-third of its total (55,148 [excluding Canada] out of 150,381). Although Europe comprised the majority of this foreign business, NYLIC also sold policies in parts of South and Central America, in Asia, and throughout the British empire.[8] At the Paris Exposition in 1889, NYLIC's display included posters that displayed its assets, with the primary poster boasting,

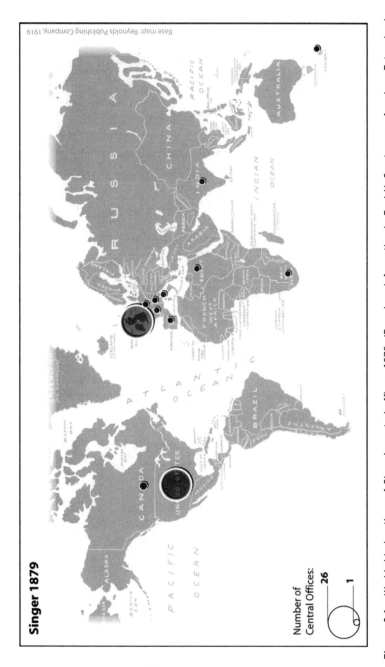

Figure 2.1 Worldwide locations of Singer's central offices, 1879. (Based on information in Fred V. Carstensen, *American Enterprise in Foreign Markets: Studies of Singer and International Harvester in Imperial Russia* [Chapel Hill, NC: University of North Carolina Press, 1984].)

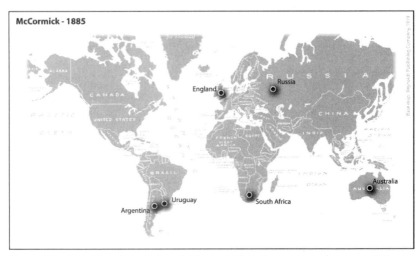

Figure 2.2   Countries where McCormick had established a structure of contracted agents, 1885. (Based on information in Fred V. Carstensen, *American Enterprise in Foreign Markets: Studies of Singer and International Harvester in Imperial Russia* [Chapel Hill, NC: University of North Carolina Press, 1984].)

"This company has branch offices in all civilized countries." Dotting these posters were small flags of certain of those countries, including the United States, France, Switzerland, Great Britain, Portugal, Australia, Italy, Norway, Mexico, Russia, Austria, Holland, Denmark, and Belgium.[9] H.J. Heinz Company began selling products in England in the late 1880s but made no major forays into foreign markets until the late 1890s. Eastman Kodak, too, began its overseas expansion in England, opening a retail shop in London in 1885 and, from there, establishing contact with agents in France, Germany, South Africa, Australia, New Zealand, India, China, and Japan.[10]

McCormick began to enter foreign markets in the late 1870s, but these were only tentative ventures, primarily in European countries such as France, Germany and Russia. By 1885, however, the company established contract agreements with agents to sell some of their equipment in England, Australia, Uruguay, South Africa, Argentina and Russia (see Figure 2.2).[11] In its 1889 catalog, the company included representations of its machines in use in a diverse array of places, including, in addition to the countries mentioned above, Mexico, Holland, North Africa, India, and Italy. And although one can surmise from this catalog that McCormick was indeed selling some of its machines in such diverse places through foreign agencies or commission houses, it is doubtful if these constituted any significant amount of business. For example, Table 2.1 indicates the value of

Table 2.1 Value of Farm Machinery (in dollars) Exported from the United States, 1892

France	Germany	Russia	Canada
345,086	222,261	81,733	43,465

Source: "Foreign Trade, Exports of American Farm Implements," Dun's Review, 1903, 11–12.

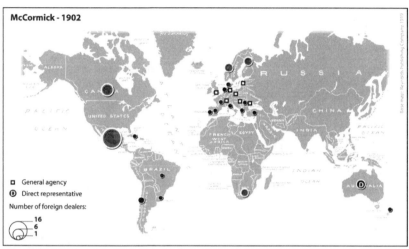

Figure 2.3 Global distribution of McCormick's foreign dealers, 1902. (The Sales Organization, July 2, 1902 [unpublished document]. Wisconsin Historical Society, McCormick-International Harvester Collection.)

farm machinery in general (not just McCormick machines, although McCormick was the largest exporter) exported to different countries in 1892.[12] Presumably, this represents a trend similar to the situation of 1889 — foreign sales represented a relatively small percentage of trade, and much of that trade was to Western Europe.

Consolidating an Empire: 1890–1915

McCormick's foreign sales increased dramatically in the last decade of the 19th century and the first several years of the 20th century, comprising an estimated 15% to 20% of the company's business.[13] As Figure 2.3 suggests, the spatial extent of McCormick's sales network also increased, particularly outside Western Europe. In addition to McCormick's general agencies in Hamburg, London, Berlin, Odessa, Riga, Budapest, and Zurich, a number of foreign dealers sold McCormick machines (see Table 2.2).

Table 2.2 Number of McCormick Dealers in Foreign Countries, in Addition to Its General Agencies in Hamburg, London, Berlin, Odessa, Riga, Budapest, and Zurich, 1902

Mexico	16	Holland	1
Australia	4	Denmark	1
South Africa	3	Turkey	1
Finland	3	Italy	1
Norway	3	Spain	1
Chile	2	Roumania	1
Brazil	1	Portugal	1
Uruguay	1	Greece	1
Cuba	1	France	1
New Zealand	1		

Source: *The Sales Organization,* July 2, 1902. [unpublished document]. Wisconsin Historical Society, McCormick-International Harvester Collection.

This spatial expanse and extent continued throughout the first decade of the 20th century. Importantly, the company merged in 1902 with four of its main competitors to form International Harvester Company, a huge conglomerate that controlled 85% of the total production of harvesting machines.[14] By 1910, foreign sales of IH machinery, twine, and other farm implements comprised more than one-third of the company's entire sales. In addition, foreign trade had increased 21.5% over the previous year, compared to an only 12.8% increase in domestic trade.[15] The company estimated that more than 28% of its profits in 1908 came from European business.[16]

At the turn of the century, with increasing European business, high tariffs, and the need to protect patent rights,[17] IH decided to open foreign manufacturing plants. Its first plant was in Norrköping, Sweden; it was purchased in 1905 and operated from 1906 on, followed 2 years later by plants in Croix, France, and Neuss, Germany. In 1910, IH opened a plant in Lubertzy, a suburb of Moscow. The company listed the value of its gross sales overseas in 1912 as $51 million, compared to $64 million for domestic sales; thus, foreign sales accounted for almost 45% of IH's overall sales.[18] By 1914, IH was a large, multinational company that owned and managed foreign manufacturing plants, resources, offices, and retail shops (see Figure 2.4) and operated 159 foreign branch offices and distributions sites around the world (see Table 2.3).

Like Singer and McCormick, Kodak began its overseas expansion in Western Europe, establishing its first foreign office in London in 1885 and then opening branch offices in Paris in 1891 and Berlin in 1896. From there, the company expanded its sales offices throughout

Table 2.3   Number of IH Foreign Branch Offices and Distribution Sites, 1914

Russia	24	Holland	3
South America	19	Roumania	3
Canada	17	Belgium	2
Africa	12	Sweden	2
Germany	8	Switzerland	2
Mexico	7	Asia Minor	2
Australia	6	China	2
Great Britain	6	Syria	2
Italy	5	Turkey	2
France	5	Denmark	1
Spain	5	Portugal	1
New Zealand	4	Serbia	1
Austria-Hungary	4	India	1
Bulgaria	4	Japan	1
Greece	3	Philippines	1
Norway	3	Siam	1
Total			**159**

Source: *Location of Foreign Branch Offices and Principal Distribution Points*
[unpublished document], 1914. Wisconsin Historical Society,
McCormick-International Harvester Collection.

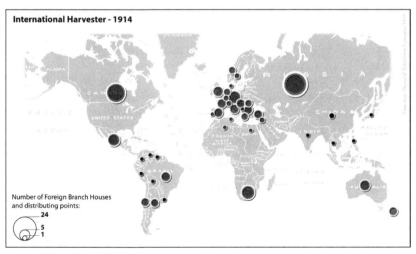

Figure 2.4   Global distribution of International Harvester's foreign branch houses and distribution points, 1914. (*Location of Foreign Branch Offices and Principal Distribution Points,* 1914 [unpublished document]. Wisconsin Historical Society, McCormick-International Harvester Collection.)

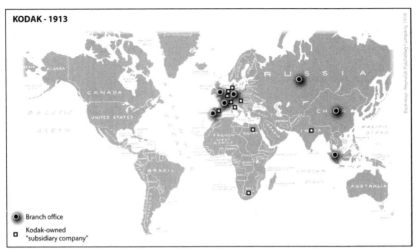

Figure 2.5 Location of Kodak's branch offices and subsidiary companies outside the United States and Canada, 1913. (*When Kodak Started to Do Business Directly in Each Country* [unpublished document]; *Russian Stores* [unpublished document]; Letter from F.C. Mattison, Managing Director of Kodak Unlimited in London, to R. Speth, July 19, 1921. All from Eastman Kodak Company, Business Information Center, Rochester, NY.)

much of Europe, either through the establishment of subsidiary companies or by establishing branch offices. Between 1905 and 1913, Kodak set up local companies in Italy, Austria, Belgium, Switzerland, Denmark, Egypt, Germany, Holland, Spain, South Africa, and India and continued its branch offices in Russia, China, Portugal, and Singapore (see Figure 2.5).[19] It also established manufacturing plants in England, France, Canada, and Australia. Although comparative statistics are not available, Kodak's foreign commerce clearly accounted for a significant percentage of its business by the first decade of the 20th century. Sales of Kodak Limited, the subsidiary company that controlled much of Kodak's foreign business, totaled $7 million for the year ending June 30, 1911.[20]

Heinz also considerably expanded its foreign markets throughout the first decade of the 20th century through the establishment of distributing branches and agencies. In 1899, the company reported, in addition to its branch house in London, distribution agencies in Toronto and Montreal; Bluefields, Nicaragua; Buenos Aires, Argentina; Liverpool, England; Bermuda; the West Indies; and Mexico City (see Figure 2.6).[21] By 1904, Heinz's sales extended to South Africa, Australia, New Zealand, the Philippines, China, Japan, and South America, and in 1906, the company reported agencies selling their products in central Africa, Thailand, Ceylon, Singapore, and Java.[22]

Figure 2.6   Location of Heinz's foreign distribution agents, 1899. ("Three Decades," *Pickles*, vol. 3, no. 4 (June 1899). H.J. Heinz Company, Pittsburgh, PA)

NYLIC continued to expand the number of policies it wrote in Europe, South America, and Asia throughout the last decades of the 19th century. In 1893, the company reported that almost 29% of its insurance in force (measured in dollar amounts) was outside theUnited States and Canada: 12% in its Spanish-American department (which included Mexico and Central and South America); 12% in continental Europe; 2% in Great Britain and Ireland; 1% in Australia; and 1% in all other countries.[23] By 1903, business expanded into Asia and Africa, with the company reporting 57 departments or branches in Europe, including Russia; 26 offices in Asia, including Vietnam, Japan, and China; 17 in South America; and 7 in Africa (see Figure 2.7).[24] By 1907, the company had 205,607 policies (out of a total of 982,448 policies) in force in foreign countries outside of Canada, approximately one-fifth of its business, a figure that stayed relatively the same until the outbreak of war in Europe in 1914 forced NYLIC to withdraw from many European markets.[25]

Singer's expansion throughout Europe and other markets continued unabated into the 20th century. A 1906 directory of shops where Singer machines were being sold throughout the world indicates the spatial expanse of its overseas sales (see Table 2.4 and Figure 2.8). At the same time, the company employed a sales force of 61,444 personnel and produced more than 1,250,000 sewing machines annually; of these, well over two-thirds were sold overseas.[26] By 1912, Singer manufactured an estimated 60% of all domestic sewing machines in use in the United States and 90% of all machines in foreign markets. Like

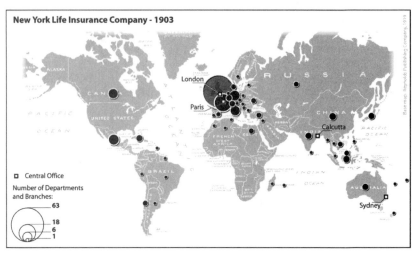

Figure 2.7   Distribution of New York Life Insurance Company's foreign departments and branches, 1903. (*Agent's Handbook*, 1903 [unpublished document]. New York Life Insurance Company Archives, The History Factory, Chantilly, VA)

Table 2.4   Number of Shops Selling Singer Sewing Machines by Country/Region, 1906

U.S. and Canada	1,359	Holland	55
Russia	754	Belgium	50
Germany	644	Sweden	36
British Isles	619	Switzerland	34
South and Central America	436	Portugal	33
Turkey	339	Hungary	24
Mexico	305	Denmark	13
Italy	238	South Africa	12
France	220	Norway	6
India	141	Philippines	1
Spain	130	Mauritius	1
Australia	109		

Source: *Directory of Shops for the Sale of Singer Sewing Machines through-out the World* [unpublished manuscript]. Wisconsin Historical Society, Singer Collection.

Kodak, Singer reacted to increasing European nationalism, tariffs, and tax complications by establishing subsidiary companies in several countries (including Russia, England, Sweden, Denmark, Norway, and Belgium).[27] In addition to increasing its foreign sales numbers,

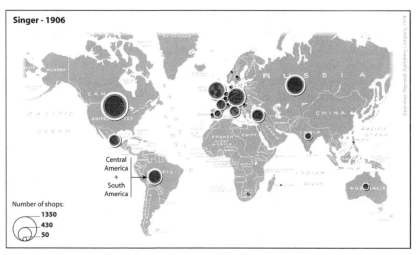

Figure 2.8   Global distribution of Singer Sewing Machine Company's retail shops, 1906. (*Directory of Shops for the Sale of Singer Sewing Machines throughout the World*, 1906 [unpublished document]. Wisconsin Historical Society, Singer Collection)

the company built two more manufacturing plants in Europe, one in Podolsk, outside of Moscow, in 1902, and one in Wittenberg, Germany, in 1904.[28] With the addition of its two factories in Canada and its largest plant in Kilbowie, Scotland, Singer had five large manufacturing concerns outside of the United States. By 1914, Singer could boast of a truly international status, both in terms of its sales organization and extent and its manufacturing and shipping enterprises.

Selling Overseas: Singer's Marketing Network

As the first and largest American international company, measured both in terms of spatial expanse and percentage of overseas sales, Singer Company was the first to face the challenges of moving, selling, and servicing its products in places very distant from its base. With an "empire" that stretched throughout the United States, Europe, and parts of Africa and Asia, including all of India, Singer required a system that was stable and consistent in order to maintain control and efficiency on the one hand, yet flexible enough to adapt to local conditions on the other. Business historians Robert Bruce Davies's and Fred Carstensen's[29] previous studies of Singer's marketing strategies make clear the relationships between the type of management policies the company developed and the spatial extent of its overseas expansion. I draw on these works in order to show how Singer produced not only machines but also spaces, creating commercial landscapes, both rural and urban, that were organized around market principles devised in the corporate boardroom in New York. By rearranging space according to market ideas and treating foreign peoples as potential consumers, Singer Manufacturing Company laid much of the groundwork for American commercial imperialism. Singer imposed its notions of economic spatiality onto landscapes around the world but learned to "temper" that imposition to fit the needs of local areas and cultures.

As Carstensen suggests,[30] before 1890, Singer's multinational successes were based primarily on expansion in industrialized nations, such as Canada, England, France, and Germany. Its sales systems had evolved through several stages; in the earliest years, before 1856, with the company short on capital and experience, it extended markets spatially primarily by selling rights to its sales to other, third-party businesses. From about 1856 to 1873, Singer developed a more mature system, under which it directly controlled more of its own sales; it bought back the territorial monopolies, expanded its construction of company-owned branch stores in major markets, and extended into secondary markets by granting exclusive rights to sell its products to particular agents. After 1873 or so, the company moved to a directly controlled, sales-intensive, and spatially extensive system by developing a network of district offices, from which a series of door-to-door canvassers "worked" the territory.

By 1890, Singer machines were primarily sold by company employees, and those sales constituted about 80% of the sales of sewing machines worldwide.[31] Here's how the system was hierarchically arranged: machines were sold by a cadre of salesmen, or "canvassers" as they were called, who were assigned areas within a district to ply their goods on a door-to-door basis. A separate group of men, called "collectors," visited each household or business weekly to collect the installment payments. This field staff worked out of district offices located in villages or towns. Most of these district offices served as retail stores and also employed an instructor who offered sewing lessons on the machines and mechanics to inspect new machines and fix old ones. These offices were overseen by an office manager, who each week compiled the sales and collection reports, tabulated certain indexes of sales and profits, and sent these monies and reports to the central office. The central offices were responsible for and supervised the district offices within their regions — and the size of those regions varied from entire countries to regions within countries. The controlling central offices reported to one of three controlling offices, located in New York, London, and Hamburg. The controlling offices in turn reported to the executives of the company in New York. At each stage, reports of sales and performance were indexed and monitored for the particular spatial area under supervision — either the district, the region, or the controlling region. In this way, those at the top, in New York, could monitor on a weekly basis the performance of their sales within their entire "empire." To provide some sense of scale, in 1880, Singer had 25 American central offices that supervised 530 district offices; the London controlling office had 26 central offices reporting to it to serve the British Isles; and the company also had central offices in Paris, Madrid, Brussels, Milan, Basel, Capetown, Bombay, Auckland, and Cairo.[32]

Exactly how these areas were divided into regions and districts varied from place to place and through time. In 1878, the company printed a circular that went to all employees laying out their recommendations for how the branch office system should work. According to this document, district offices were to be located in the largest towns within the territory of the central office, with the minimum population threshold of the area served by these offices set at 5,000 people. These offices were to be located within the downtown business district and were to be rented. If a particular region was large enough that canvassing from one of the district offices was not feasible, then a suboffice was to be established, under the direct control of the district office. In cases where there was not enough business to merit the establishment of these suboffices, then a station agent was hired who paid his own expenses and traveled with his own horse and wagon. As Davies explains, "this one man operation was the lowest level of Singer's sales organization."[33]

Each canvasser was assigned six particular routes within the district, one for each working day of the week. Depending on the region, the canvasser also served as the collector, so his weekly visitations were to prompt new sales, collect weekly payments, and service machines if necessary. Canvassers were paid a fixed salary plus commissions on sales and collections. The regularity with which these men canvassed the area meant that they became a familiar sight and, according to Davies, "would be known to every family on his route."[34] The canvassers were thought to be the key to sales success; they were meant to be energetic, bright, knowledgeable about the machines, and honest. Most of these canvassers were "natives" — that is, although as one moved up the hierarchy at Singer, the employees became more American and white, at the base of that hierarchy, the company employed local peoples. Singer realized that canvassers needed to know not only the local language but also the cultural norms and social mores that guided peoples' lives.

The Russian market provided a challenge to Singer, particularly in terms of its spatial expanse and rurality. Machines were first sold (in the 1860s and early 1870s) through agents who had offices in key cities, but sales were not brisk. By the late 1870s, the company decided to move more directly into sales and send their own representatives to tour the country and establish company stores in major markets; at the same time, they offered contracts to agents in secondary markets to sell their goods, thus establishing brand name recognition in these markets and laying the groundwork for future expansion of Singer offices. Primary offices were built in St. Petersburg, Warsaw, and Moscow. By 1894, the company had expanded drastically. From the Moscow office alone, the company supervised 20 large retail stores and 50 smaller stores, and they employed 70 agents, 50 clerks, 75 saleswomen, 280 collectors and town travelers, 275 country travelers, and 135 mechanics and packers.[35] In 1895, the company sold 68,788 machines in Russia.[36] With its failures in sales in China, Singer's executives saw this new Russian market as a solution to its almost saturated markets in the United States and Western Europe. President Bourne told his American stockholders in 1898 that the opportunities in Russia were "tremendous."[37]

The company also decided that Russia required its own subsidiary organization and, in 1897, they established a joint stock Russian company — Kompaniya Singer — with headquarters in a new and noteworthy building on the main street in the heart of St. Petersburg. At this point, the company had four central offices in Russia — in Moscow, St. Petersburg, Riga, and Warsaw — with each office supervising large district retail stores. The Moscow region had 21 district offices, Warsaw and St. Petersburg had 9 offices each, and the Riga region contained 6 district offices. By 1899, the country contained more than 100 Singer retail stores.[38]

Sales of machines in Russia increased dramatically throughout the first decade of the 20th century, more than doubling between 1900 (over 110,000 machines sold) and 1905 (over 310,000 machines sold), with a similar growth rate in the next 10 years, jumping in 1914 to total sales of 678,986 machines.[39] This growth in sales was primarily the result of making machines available and affordable to such a large population, thus not requiring the heavy-handed marketing and advertising campaigns that were used in the United States. Singer therefore put its energies into two areas: expanding the spatial extent of its sales apparatus, thus physically enabling its products to reach customers, and maintaining vigilance over the collection of weekly payments. In other words, Singer realized that Russians would buy the machines if they were available and affordable.

However, Russian political and economic conditions were different from those of most of the other countries where Singer had successfully organized overseas sales networks; specifically, most Russian people were significantly poorer than their Western European neighbors. Singer estimated that the value of one Singer machine in 1900 (Rs. 74.40) was more than the Russian average annual per capita income (Rs. 70). Because of this, the company had to change some of its sales practices and policies. The normal practice of employing both canvassers and collectors — that is, one group of personnel whose responsibilities were for sales and a separate group whose responsibilities were for collections — was not viable in Russia. The number of sales per area simply didn't merit the pay for two employees to cover the same region. Instead, the company decided to place both responsibilities in the hands of canvasser/collectors and rewarded these people with commissions that were geared more to the collection of payments than to new sales. By shifting the emphasis to collections rather than new sales, the company recognized the particular economic and geographic conditions of Russia. The company didn't charge interest on these credit payments; instead, they significantly raised the price of the machines. It adapted its practices in other ways as well. The company made provisions for customers who couldn't pay the initial down payment of Rs. 10, and they extended the time allotted to pay off the machine, from the "normal" 2 years to 4 years, thus allowing families to significantly reduce their weekly payments These adaptations to the "local" socioeconomic conditions coincided with adaptations to the spatial scale of the Russian nation. Because of the expanse of territory that had to be covered, more than half of Singer's agents in Russia worked "semiautonomously" because they operated at great distances from their supervisory offices and "made only weekly visits to submit reports."[40] Those agents working in more remote areas only reported once every 2 weeks, and those in Siberia and Central Asia reported to their central office even less frequently.[41]

Maintaining supervision over this spatially extensive system was a challenging task, one that required Singer to rework the "normal" accounting system that it had used in Western Europe and the United States. First, the company established a new "reporting" hierarchy. It grouped canvasser/collectors into what it called "depots," or groups, each composed of about six agents. These depots — up to 40 of them — were then grouped together and supervised by a central office. Second, it limited the number of accounts maintained at each level. For example, each canvasser/collector was limited to 100 accounts, and the depots were divided into two types dependent on conditions, one that supervised no more than 800 accounts and 8 agents and another that supervised no more than 25 agents, and therefore 2,500 accounts. The central office was in charge of no more than 40 depots, or up to 60,000 accounts. In this system, then, growth occurred not within each division but by establishing new depots. At the level of the individual salesperson, therefore, money was made not necessarily by increasing sales but by maintaining collections. The system also worked to ensure that each salesperson maintained a close relationship with those 100 accounts and therefore with a particular geographical area. When growth happened, it was expressed through an expansion of the system — that is, another canvasser would be hired to work another district. Thus, as sales rose, the country was divided into smaller and smaller districts. Third, the company's system of submitting weekly written reports at each level of the hierarchy meant that communication and supervision was maintained at short time intervals. Assessments of sales, collections, and profits could be tabulated weekly, allowing adjustments in the system to be made quite rapidly. And fourth, the central office manager, along with his assistant manager, auditors, and other supervisory personnel, were constantly on the move, traveling throughout the part of the country under their supervision.[42] These travels were conducted monthly, although not all depots were visited each month. After these supervisory visits, and after compiling the reports received from each depot, the central office manager compiled a monthly report that was sent to the Russian headquarters in St. Petersburg. The staff in St. Petersburg had their own set of auditors who made visits to each central office. Offices that showed signs of decreased collections, excessive expenses, or other problems were targeted for longer visits, sometimes lasting several weeks, during which the problems were assessed and changes were made to procedure or staff. The reports of these inspections, along with regular monthly reports of sales and collections, were then forwarded to Singer's main office in New York. If problems persisted, staff from the New York office were sometimes sent to accompany St. Petersburg staff on visits to central offices.

This reporting system allowed the company to know exactly what was going on economically at each level of their marketing network and to make quick adjustments to their system, if necessary. It was also, of course, extremely costly. The emphasis on maintaining small units where person-to-person communication was the key to collections and on constant travel by both the canvassers and supervisory managers meant that Singer had created a system with large costs for salaries, commissions, and traveling expenses. In addition, because each depot required its own building and staff and growth in sales led not to larger areas reporting to each depot but rather to an increase in the number of depots, Singers' expenses increased along with that growth. A controlled but flexible marketing network, particularly in a place as large as Russia, was a very expensive proposition.

This spatial and organizational structure of Singer in Russia paralleled what Singer had produced in most of its other European markets, although the scale of the structure was much larger. However, as Carstensen points out, "Singer's desire for standardization conflicted with the particular needs and environment of Russia."[43] Singer Company's resolution to this conflict involved accommodations to their standard structure, accommodations that related to the country's size and economic formation. Albert Flohr, head of the St. Petersburg office, initiated several procedural changes in the first decade of the 20th century. Some of those changes related to the relationship between the individual sales agent and the company. In most instances, Singer had insisted that agents themselves put up a certain amount of capital in a reserve fund to cover any potential embezzlement; however, Flohr recognized that most Russians did not have access to that amount of capital, and so he devised a different system of "insurance."

More interestingly, Singer executives found that they needed to be flexible in terms of their spatial organization and business operations. The necessity of personnel from the central offices to make visits to each depot was a problem for managers in districts where that travel involved long distances in uncomfortable wagons, such as those in Eastern Russia and Siberia. The manager of the Omsk central region, for example, faced a situation in which many of his depots were located several hundred kilometers from the rail lines. In addition, payment structure had to be altered to fit the economic situation of nomadic peoples. Carstensen quotes the Omsk manager's account from 1907:

> Among our customers here [Petropavlovsk depot] there are a large number of Kirgeeses [Kirzhiz] who lead a nomad life, so they are irregular payers, without being bad or unworthy of credit. Yet these people have cash only at the time of the yearly markets, while at other times the agent is frequently obliged to take cattle in place of money.... Our agent can hardly avoid trading or bartering here, as buyers in very many cases have no cash at disposal, but for their goods, i.e. cattle, pelts, or fish, [they] make exchanges with the merchants for the necessary products; ... Our agent is thus obliged in many cases to take these goods and sell them for his own account.[44]

Singer agents therefore were not averse to bartering for their machines, a practice that Carstensen speculates was encouraged by Singer, which adapted its system of installment payments to fit the barter economy.

In Irkutsk, Siberia, Singer adapted its sales techniques to fit local conditions of transport. Because rivers formed the main transport arteries, Singer agents joined other merchants in forming a series of barges that carried products that were leashed together and moved downstream along the rivers, a sort of floating marketplace. A Singer agent in Siberia explained it thus: "On the way every place [was] stopped at and worked, where this [appeared] to be measurably profitable; the remainder of the goods [was] then brought to the destination and given to an agent."[45] According to Carstensen, this became a "normal" way that Singer's business expanded in Siberia — training an agent and then floating him and his goods downriver to a new destination.

In terms of overall sales, these adaptations paid off. Singer's sales figures of 1909 show that the company sold almost 500,000 machines per year, a number that far exceeded its sales of 1900.[46] Albert Flohr thought further expansion was possible and initiated some organizational changes to accommodate that growth. Siberia was of particular concern to him; he figured it was still prime territory for future growth, yet its size and overall distance from headquarters required some special considerations. In 1910, Flohr introduced a new level of management — an office that would supervise several of the centrals in eastern Russia, in effect then overseeing a large chunk of Russia and reporting directly to headquarters. This office was located in Samara and included the centrals of Samara, Orenburg, Omsk, Tomsk, Irkutsk, and Vladivostok. Another regional office was established in St. Petersburg to oversee the northwest area, and in 1914, a third regional office was established in Kharkov, Ukraine, to supervise the centrals in South Russia.[47] Apparently, the growth in the number of centrals and the increasing number of shops and offices necessitated the introduction of these new regional offices. This growth, combined with the scale of territory in which Kompaniya Singer operated, necessitated another fundamental change: Singer management decided to move their headquarters from St. Petersburg to Moscow, which was more centrally located. The company moved into a building in the old city of Moscow that was almost twice as large as their former headquarters in St. Petersburg, now rented to the Russian-English bank. By 1914, these changes were all in place and Singer's business "empire" in Russia was consolidated: headquarters in Moscow, 3 regional offices, 50 centrals, approximately 4,000 depots and stores, and 27,439 employees with almost 700,000 machines sold, a number that almost rivaled the sales in the United States, which totaled 900,000.[48]

Kompaniya Singer's success was partly due then to this immense organizational structure that managed to maintain adequate control over vast amounts of space. Weekly reports filed by canvasser/collectors in far eastern Siberia were tabulated and overseen by managers at depots, who then reported to central offices, to regional offices, to headquarters in Moscow, with tabulations reaching Singer's top management in New York within weeks. At the most local level, the Singer "man" on horseback was a common, everyday sight. In towns of significant size, shops introduced customers to new machines and employees provided lessons on how to use them. Larger cities had central offices where middle managers tabulated and planned, while the headquarter building in Moscow symbolically and functionally oversaw the country's sales operations. Each level of the hierarchy of course also contained all the services below it — in other words, central offices also operated stores and oversaw canvassers, just as regional offices contained all the functions of central offices, and so forth.[49]

At each level of the hierarchy, then, different types of activities and social interactions took place. As previously mentioned, the canvasser/collector was the person with the most daily contact with customers. In Russia, as in most of Singer's other foreign markets, most of these canvassers were "native" people, drawn from the surrounding area. In rural areas, this person took daily horseback rides through the countryside, visiting farms and small villages. He (they were all men) carried with him samples of Singer's various machines and the materials necessary to demonstrate their use, such as thread and fabric. He also carried with him his notebook, where he marked the weekly payments that he did or did not collect. He interacted with customers mainly in their own homes, a visitor of sorts, perhaps known by the family beforehand or at least familiar to them by name and relations. This was a commercial interaction, but one that was also personal and friendly and one that took place in the private spaces of home. In many cases, the fact that the product was American — whatever that meant — was not part of the conversation. Many of the machines, in fact, were produced in Russia at Singer's factory in Podolsk, just outside of Moscow. Although decorated with the Singer logo, these machines were stamped with the Kompaniya Singer mark and were sold by Russian sales agents. In other words, the personal commercial interactions at the local level were in most cases interactions that did not involve the "foreign" in any way.

The other local interactions occurred in the approximately 4,000 Singer shops that were located in towns throughout Russia. Here, potential customers could browse the various machines, examine samples of what could be made on each of them, watch demonstrations of various sewing techniques by employees, and take sewing classes. Most of the employees who worked the floor in these shops and who demonstrated and gave sewing lessons were "natives," and many of them were women. Given the historical association of sewing as women's work, Singer was simply following domestic guidelines in hiring women to demonstrate and teach about their products. No women were hired at any level above retail sales and sewing instructors.

Each of the sales offices and stores collected detailed information about the general economic well-being of its population base. This was particularly importance given that approximately 90% of all sales in Russia were on an installment plan. Local knowledge of, for example, a bad harvest year or labor dispute at the main factory in town was needed to assess potential credit risks. Therefore, retail employees were familiar with the general economic statuses of their potential customers. Once a sale had been made and the customer had paid the down payment, the machine was not delivered until a full credit investigation had been completed and the company could reasonably expect their weekly payments.[50] What exactly was involved in this "investigation" is not clear; presumably, a Singer staff member drawn from the local population, and therefore with access to local knowledge, made visits and phone calls to financial institutions and other local institutions. After the appropriate information had been obtained, the machine was delivered and regular weekly payments were either collected or brought to the store or office.

The "localness" of these types of interactions changed as soon as an employee moved up the Singer hierarchy. As previously mentioned, most of the canvassers, collectors, and sales staff on the "floor" were drawn from the local population; the managers and auditors who oversaw their work, and everyone else up the ladder, came from other places. Many of these employees were drawn from other parts of Singer's "empire," mainly England and Germany. They also were recruited from ethnic minorities living in Russia, particularly ethnic Germans and Jews. For example, in the Kiev, Odessa, and Kozlovo offices, nearly all employees were Jewish.[51] The reliance on German managers is partly explained by the fact that the first head of Singer operations in Russia was Neidlinger, who himself was German and had formerly managed the Hamburg office. He brought with him to Russia many of his colleagues and continued to "mine" the Hamburg office and other centrals in Germany and Austria for capable and ambitious men willing to move to Russia. According to Carstensen, this reliance on foreign managers also reflected a lack of commercial

and entrepreneurial background amongst the general Russian population. In other words, Singer did not necessarily want to hire out-
siders but found after much trial and error that they needed to rely
on nonethnic Russian help. As Carstensen suggests, "[this hierarchy]
developed not out of choice but out of necessity and reflected the
difficulties of finding people with sufficient commercial experience
and ability in Russia."[52] Interactions within local sales offices and
stores, then, often involved relationships between local employees,
who worked directly with customers, and their managers and auditors, who often spoke a different language or were from a foreign
country. Most of the managers of the central offices were foreigners;
and of the 47 people who worked at headquarters in Moscow, 13
were from Germany or Austria, and they occupied all the important
positions.[53]

Singer's successful sales and administrative structure in Russia
consisted of the hierarchical and tightly controlled spatial system
developed in New York, an administrative structure reliant on Western European employees and expertise, and a network of "native"
workers with local knowledge necessary to conduct credit checks and
surveillance of potential customers. For Singer, the Russian population provided a large source of potential sales for the machines, but
not necessarily of entrepreneurial skills. Singer's system of sales was
adapted to fit these conditions (by importing mangers), but its expansion otherwise moved along without any formidable obstacles from
"local conditions."

In other foreign markets outside of Western Europe, Singer was
forced to make more significant adaptations. India, with its large population base and British rulers, was at first glance a potentially large
market for Singer. In 1875, George Woodruff, Singer's "main man" in
their London office assigned to the development of sales in the British
empire, appointed Nusserwanjee Merwanjee Patell as Singer's agent to
Bombay.[54] Patell, like most of Singer's other employees in India, was
a Parsee — an ethnic minority in India who traced their roots to pre-
Muslim Persia and who had a long history as a class of successful merchants and entrepreneurs. Although "local" in the sense of geographical and historical attachment to India, particularly the Bombay area,
Parsees were neither Hindi nor Muslim and formed a small but elite
group, a group that served as intermediaries under British rule. Sales
of machines were very small in the first years, but Woodruff thought
Patell was doing a good job and was "an honest man."[55] Although
Woodruff originally divided the country into a northern half run from
Calcutta and a southern half run from Bombay, in 1881, he made
Patell the general agent for Singer in the entire country.[56]

But from the first years, Singer representatives realized the difficulties that India presented to market expansion. For example, in 1888, a company inspector named Mitchell from the London office visited India and Patell's operation. His letters back to the London office reveal a long list of problems: that native women were secluded and uneducated; that "if advertisements reached their hands they would be unable to understand them";[57] that because of caste issues, homes generally would not be accessible to company canvassers; that Indians in general did not approve of credit payments; and that Indian clothing styles did not require sewing machines, something that would limit the market to only Europeans and Anglos living in India, who comprised a tiny fraction of the population.[58] Yet despite hints of these problems in the early 1880s, Singer management at first considered them only temporary obstacles that could be removed with persistence and adequate management.

When Patell's sales records did not soar within the first 5 years or so, Singer sent out investigators to visit and report on the situation. Patell apparently had failed to hire any canvassers, employing only minimal sales staff at his Bombay and Calcutta offices. The investigator's solution to the caste issue was to hire canvassers from each class, who would then be able to visit the homes of their peers. To implement these changes, an assistant from the London office, Duncan Davidson, was sent to work with Patell. Davidson instituted the "normal" system of canvassers in towns along the Indus River, including Karachi and Hyderabad, but this failed to produce any results. Patell was fired in June of 1887 but was subsequently rehired in October and given more flexibility in arranging his sales force. Woodruff concluded that Singer should not try to rigidly impose on other countries the sales system it had developed within the United States and Europe and that the company should consider India "from local points of view."[59] Thus, when John Mitchell was sent to help Patell in 1888, he came with instructions to adapt and not impose the English system. Mitchell observed that most customers preferred to buy at a shop and pay in cash — quite different from Singer's experiences of selling through canvassers with credit arrangements. Therefore, he helped institute resident agents instead of canvassers who, in different cities, would advertise and take orders for new machines.

This more nuanced approach to conducting business in India continued through the next decade. Vice-President Alexander wrote to Patell in 1902 that he need not worry about adopting "all these forms word for word and line for line" but instead could alter them in ways that would best fit his "exact requirements."[60] With this new approach, Singer's sales rose, but never quite matched what the New

York office had originally thought for a country the size of India. In 1901, the company sold 13,352 machines through its 22 district offices and 81 suboffices, better by far than any of its competitors, but a small number given India's population of 200 million people.[61] In both Russia and India, therefore, Singer Company was faced with "local conditions" (i.e., different cultures) that required it to adapt its sales methods and management styles. In doing so, they created "hybrid spaces" — stores and offices — where both American "ways" of business and local cultures of commerce came together. In Russia, they transformed the most common of spaces — people's homes — into commercialized spaces, albeit only temporarily, when canvassers visited on their weekly rounds. Singer Company succeeded in its international sales efforts through its flexible approach to commerce and culture.

Manufacturing Overseas: McCormick/IH's Foreign Plants

IH devoted years of research and discussion to the question of whether and how they should construct manufacturing plants overseas. As early as 1903, company executives investigated the possibility of buying or constructing a foreign manufacturing plant. Instructions given by Vice President Harold McCormick to the company's employee W. Krebs before his trip abroad to investigate these possibilities is telling of their immediate concerns. First, McCormick instructs him to collect data on the company's competitors: their names and locations, their financial standing, the number and types of machines they produce, and their costs in terms of raw materials, wages, shipping, and the like. Second, he lists the important factors that Krebs should include in his investigations in each country: 1) "to ascertain what concessions or other benefits, if any, the American manufacturers receive to induce them to build abroad, 2) cost of labor and general labor situation, 3) cost of raw material, 4) traffic facilities and rates, 5) taxes, insurance, etc." He also mentions "a very important matter, which has a direct present bearing upon this Company, viz: the tariff."[62] These concerns indicate both the "normal" issues facing any locational decisions for manufacturing plants (costs of labor, raw materials, and transportation) and two additional concerns caused by the internationalism of these decisions — concessions to American businesses and tariffs.

These diverse issues were investigated in detail for several years, with different groups of company employees being sent out from the main Chicago office to visit, ask questions, and send back reports from possible site locations. Not all the reports agreed on the issues. One of the most interesting questions the company faced was whether they should think of building plants to serve the needs of one country or region, or whether they should look for one large, central plant that could produce machines for the entire European market. Because one of the primary motives for investing in a foreign manufacturing plant was to avoid tariffs on the import of American products, the danger of the second solution was that it was probable that countries would enact similar tariffs on products manufactured in other European states. In other words, IH could be spending large sums of money to produce machines overseas in order to avoid tariffs, only to find similar tariffs cutting into their profits as they shipped, say, harvesters made in France to Sweden, or vice versa. As one company representative put it: "The paramount consideration in Europe is the possibility of the tariff which any country is almost as likely to place on goods manufactured in Germany, France, or Sweden, as against those manufactured in the United States."[63] On the other hand, building different plants in each country that comprised a large share of IH's market was very costly and perhaps unnecessarily duplicative.

As European countries became more protective of their own manufacturing interests with increased tariffs, IH proceeded on the first option, moving slowly and assessing each market separately. Sweden was their first target, where the company purchased an already-established factory in Norrköping in 1905 and turned it into a plant for the manufacture of grass-harvesting machines. Their interests here were sparked by the competition of a Swedish company, Arvika, that was selling cheaper machines, and by the generally-recognized fact that, unlike farmers in some other European countries, Swedish farmers were not willing to pay more for an American-made machine than for a locally built one.[64] The company originally considered buying Arvika, continuing a long-standing practice of horizontal integration, but the company's selling price rose so high in anticipation of the sale that IH instead bought the factory in Norrköping and converted it to its uses.[65]

In the meantime, the company continued its surveillance of the situations in Russia, Germany, and France. After Krebs' initial visits, representatives of the company provided updates on each country: the condition of local farm machinery manufacturers, the political situation vis-à-vis tariffs, and the possible locations and situations of an IH plant. One letter that provided such an update on the condition in France is particularly revealing. Dated 1905, the letter opens by stating that there had been relatively little change in the situation of French manufacturers since Krebs' visit 2 years earlier. The author of the letter, Mr. LaPorte, head of IH's Paris office, provides a brief description of each of the five firms that manufactured farm machinery — what they specialized in, their capitalization, and so forth. He then delves into a discussion of the pros and cons of constructing a factory in France. The cons include the difficulties of labor in France ("organized labor, which, although not well paid in France, is nevertheless rebellious and at this very minute there is scarcely a section of France that does not have its strikes or Labor troubles"[66]), the lack of economies of scale, and the high cost of materials, making the manufacture of machines not "enough cheaper in France at present to cover the cost of transportation and the duty." On the pro side, however, was the "fact that at any minute France may enact a retaliatory Tariff measure which will either shut us out of the French market or we shall be compelled to do business here with scarcely any profit." The United States had initiated protective tariffs that had kept most foreign manufacturers out of the country, a position that LaPorte called "the present unfair position of the United States on the Tariff question," and that would eventually "arouse the antagonism of the entire manufacturing world." The potential tariff situation, combined with other factors concerning the general state of business in France and the potential new sales there ("it is the second largest Wheat-growing country in the world") led LaPorte to conclude that France was third on his list of priorities for the company to consider, after Sweden and Russia. His views of the potential site of Russia for a factory are interesting, based mostly on Russia's potentially large market and base of resources: "It is the greatest undeveloped field in the world and has resources equal to, if not in excess of the United States when they are fully developed."[67]

Assessing the potential feasibility of tapping this "undeveloped field" in Russia was a lengthy process. On the pro side, IH knew that Russia was potentially their largest market and thought they could manufacture machines there cheaper given the high import duties and the low cost of labor. On the con side was the potential risk of investing large sums of money in a country that seemed very different culturally and economically from the United States. To lessen some of these worries, Chapman, who had been sent by IH to visit European factories in 1905, spent more than a month in Russia, sending back 23 detailed reports.[68] He was concerned particularly about the quality of Russian workers, but his visit to Singer's plant in Podolsk eased some of his concerns because the plant seemed to be running smoothly, with adequately trained Russian workers and foreman. The letter and report he sent back indicated this interest in labor: the report was divided into eight categories, five of which were concerned with labor, and the letter included a detailed accounting of the wages and quality of work within Singer's factory. Chapman writes, "Russian foreman and employees have been used from the start so that the prices were never allowed to get up to high standards by importing men from America," and "In the Packing Department a boy was making boxes or really crates as fast as anywhere. Price per 100 crates $.38-1/4. This young man gets about $.56 per day."[69] Based primarily on Chapman's report, the company executives concluded at a conference in London in August of 1905 that they should begin manufacture of Lubograkas (a simplified, Russian-style reaper) in Russia as soon as the Russian-Japanese war ended.

Company executives were uneasy, however, with operating foreign manufacturing. Sales for reapers had declined in the United States after the boom years of the late 1890s and, therefore, maintaining profit margins required making up for this gap in domestic sales by increasing the production of machines for foreign sales. This kept the factories in the United States running at capacity. Opening additional plants outside the United States, therefore, did not seem a good solution. On the other hand, the fear of increasing tariffs kept IH executives alert because such tariffs would lead to an overall decrease in overseas sales, sales that they were now increasingly reliant upon. Between 1906 and 1909, the company stalled on making any further decisions about foreign concerns. By spring of 1908, Cyrus McCormick took the matter into his own hands, realizing that improved marketing was not enough to sustain the company's share of the trade in Russia, Germany, and France. He instigated another round of investigations, sending four experts throughout Europe to analyze potential sites for foreign plants.[70] Additional reports and conferences generated by these investigations led the company board to agree to develop factories in France and Germany, but the case of Russia was left undecided. McCormick determined that he needed to see the situation firsthand and, in 1908, made a tour of Europe, visiting the company's plant in Sweden and the two new plants it had bought in France and Germany. He also planned a lengthy tour to Russia to examine potential sites for plants and to discuss matters with government officials, who he hoped would offer the company incentives to operate their plant there.

In 1909, McCormick made his way to St. Petersburg and met with the Ministers of Finance, Commerce, and Agriculture. Transcripts of these interviews reveal some of the anxieties, both on the part of the company and the Russian government, surrounding the decision to build a manufacturing plant in the country. For the company, the main issue was whether the government would support the company in formal and informal ways. Formally, McCormick wanted concessions from the government in the form of lower duties on imported parts that were needed for the plant and on machines that were brought in while the plant was under construction, tax remissions from local and state governments, and a commitment by the government to raise and maintain duties on machines that were imported (thus, in essence, eliminating International Harvester's competition).[71] Informally, the company hoped that government officials would generally support and protect the company's interests.

Being warned in advance of raising the specificities of the concessions on this first round of interviews, before the company had committed to establish a plant there, McCormick couched his concerns in very general language. Of the six general points that McCormick raised with each of the three ministers, three dealt with the need for informal government support. McCormick stated in point two that "we wish to know whether the Russian government is desirous and willing that United States capital should embark in this work," and in point three, "we wish and need the approval and the co-operation of the Russian Government and officials in every reasonable way." Point five gets even closer to what was at stake: "Personally I have favored this plan for a long time but my associates in Chicago hesitate because they feel that foreign capital might not receive this protection and encouragement which is accorded in other countries where they welcome foreign capital. I have now succeeded in convincing my associates that this is a good plan if the Russian officials and Government will give us their cordial support and assistance."[72] Clearly, what was at issue here was the degree to which Russia was different from France, Germany, and Sweden, the other countries where the company had already opened manufacturing plants. Was Russia, in other words, willing to "play ball" with American capital? If the interviews with the three ministers were any indication, the company should have felt assured of government cooperation. Of particular interest to both the Ministers of Finance and Commerce was the protection of the tariff. Both ministers favored the protection of home industries through tariffs, but no tariffs had been levied for farm machinery since the only reliable machines available in Russia at this time were imported. Thus, as Mr. Kovotsoff, Minister of Finance, stated: "Therefore those of us like myself and the Minister of Commerce and others who feel that Russia should have a tariff to encourage home industries are really in the strange position of fostering foreign industry in Agricultural machines.... Now if you come and begin manufacturing in Russia no doubt we can soon put up the tariff on Agricultural machines, as we would like to do."[73] McCormick's proposal to build a plant in Russia was beneficial to both sides: it would enable Russia to maintain its high tariff wall, and this would handicap McCormick's competition. Thus IH could be assured that the government would support its interests.

Apparently, these informal gestures of support, with no specific concessions, were enough to satisfy McCormick and other company executives. After lengthy reports and negotiations, the company finally decided in 1910 to buy an existing engine plant in Lubertzy, outside of Moscow, and use it to produce mowers, rakes, and lubograkas. Yet as Carstensen points out in his study of IH in Russia, the management of the plant, and IH's relationship with the government, were less than satisfactory. IH never did get any special concessions, and the company was never able to influence policy. Nonetheless, the plant finally became profitable, employing almost all-Russian labor — a result more of the increased sales in Russia of IH machines in the first two decades of the 20th century than of any concessions or manufacturing expertise.[74]

These two case studies — McCormick's decision-making process in locating its Russian factory and Singer's network of sales offices and canvassers — point to the flexibility of American business systems overseas. In both cases, the companies followed the locational decision-making rationale that they used at home, adapting when necessary to their local contexts. They most often hired local people (with the exception of employees at the managerial level for Singer), conducted business in local languages, and created work spaces that in many cases differed little from their local competitors. Following a similar economic logic that had propelled them west into the expanding United States, these companies learned to adapt to local circumstances as they pursued their global expansion plans. Yet, the actions of these companies reshaped the commercial landscapes of many countries in profound ways. By 1910, Singer, McCormick/IH, Heinz, Kodak, NYLIC had extensive "empires" that reached deep into the social networks of many countries, including most of Europe, parts of East and South Asia, Central and South America, Australia, and New Zealand. The construction of factories, retail shops, and office buildings, and the circulation of the commodities themselves and their advertising, brought the names of these companies and meanings associated with them into the streets and homes of cities and rural areas far from the United States. But so too this expansion brought the names of foreign places and peoples into the homes and streets of cities and rural areas *within* the United States. These early international companies used their foreign experiences as advertising tools, to boast not only of their size and popularity but also of their role as agents of civilization — that is, they associated the spatial spread of their products with missionary work, bringing modernization and civilization to "others." Because of this, verbal and visual images of these "other" peoples and places often figured prominently in the advertising and the corporate culture of these companies. In this way, representations of the world "out there" began to circulate widely within the United States, relaying a type of geography lesson. I turn now to examining the first of these geographical lessons, the ones taught through Singer's advertising.

Endnotes

1. Kevin H. O'Rourke and Jeffrey G. Williamson, *Globalization and History: The Evolution of a Nineteenth-Century Atlantic Economy* (Cambridge, MA: MIT Press, 1999), 34.
2. Ibid., 36.
3. This discursive relationship between U.S. companies and their potential consumers in other countries is clearly very different from the relationship (discursive and otherwise) between U.S. companies and their workers in other countries. See, for example, Allen Wells, *Yucatán's Gilded Age: Haciendas, Henequen, and International Harvester, 1860–1915* (Albuquerque, NM: University of New Mexico Press, 1985) and Gilbert G. González, *Culture of Empire: American Writers, Mexico, and Mexican Immigrants, 1880–1930* (Austin, TX: University of Texas Press, 2004).
4. Don Bissell, *The First Conglomerate: 145 Years of the Singer Sewing Machine Company* (Brunswick, ME: Audenreed Press, 1999), 1.
5. Ibid., 81.
6. Mira Wilkins, *The Emergence of Multinational Enterprise: American Business Abroad from the Colonial Era to 1914* (Cambridge, MA: Harvard University Press, 1970), 43; Fred V. Carstensen, *American Enterprise in Foreign Markets: Studies of Singer and International Harvester in Imperial Russia* (Chapel Hill, NC: University of North Carolina Press, 1984), 24; Robert Bruce Davies, *Peacefully Working to Conquer the World: Singer Sewing Machines in Foreign Markets, 1854–1920* (New York: Arno Press, 1976), 39.
7. Bissell (1999), 115.
8. Foreign Business Other than Canada (unpublished manuscript), NYLIC archives, History Factory, Chantilly, VA.
9. James Monroe Hudnut, *Semi-Centennial History of the New-York Life Insurance Company, 1845–1895* (New York: The Company, 1895), 261.
10. Kodak and the World Market (unpublished manuscript), Eastman Kodak Company, Business Information Center, Rochester, NY.
11. Carstensen (1984), 112.
12. "Foreign Trade, Exports of American Farm Implements," *Dun's Review*, (1903): 11–12.

13. This number is taken from Cyrus McCormick's testimony in the federal government's investigation of the formation of IH as a possible monopoly trust in 1913. When asked what percentage of business was in foreign trade prior to 1902, McCormick answered "I never figured it up ... fifteen to twenty percent." From Department of Commerce and Labor, Washington, Report on The International Harvester Co., 1913, 71.

14. Department of Commerce and Labor, 67.

15. Total sales in 1910 equaled $62,933,361.99, of which the United States comprised $37,730,447.61 and foreign countries equaled $25,202,914.38. Annual Report, International Harvester Company, 1910, 4.

16. Memo from W.W. Reay, Assistant Comptroller, to Cyrus H. McCormick, President, June 16, 1908, Wisconsin Historical Society, McCormick-International Harvester Collection.

17. In many countries, patent rights could not be protected if the product was manufactured outside the country. This enabled other companies to produce identical machines and, without tariff and transport costs, to sell them cheaper. See W.C. Caton's unpublished manuscript "Organization of International Harvester's Foreign Operations Since 1902," 1976, Wisconsin Historical Society, McCormick-International Harvester Collection.

18. Unpublished document, Wisconsin Historical Society, McCormick-International Harvester Collection.

19. When Kodak Started to Do Business Directly in Each Country (unpublished manuscript); F.C. Mattison (managing director of Kodak Limited in London) to R. Speth, July 19, 1921; Russian Stores (unpublished manuscript) (all three items are from the Business Information Center, Eastman Kodak Company).

20. Sales by Kodak Limited for One Year to June 30th, 1911 (unpublished manuscript), Business Information Center, Eastman Kodak Company.

21. "Three Decades," Pickles, 3, 4 (June 1899):

22. "Our Foreign Agencies," The 57, 8, 1 (1904): 14–17; "Trade Extension for the 57," The 57, 10, 2 (January 1906): 1–3.

23. Hudnut (1895), 356.

24. Agent's Handbook, 1903, NYLIC archives, History Factory, Chantilly, VA.

25. New York Life International Operations (unpublished manuscript), NYLIC archives, History Factory, Chantilly, VA.

26. Robert Bruce Davies, Peacefully Working to Conquer the World: Singer Sewing Machines in Foreign Markets, 1854–1920 (New York: Arno Press, 1976), 139–141.

27. Ibid., 161.

28. Ibid., 115.

29. Davies (1976); Carstensen (1984).

30. Carstensen (1984), 13–26.

31. Ibid., 23.
32. Ibid., 22.
33. Davies(1976), 61.
34. Ibid., 64.
35. Carstensen (1984), 31.
36. Ibid., 33.
37. Quote in Davies (1976), 255.
38. Carstensen (1984), 40.
39. Ibid., 56.
40. Ibid., 60.
41. Ibid., 60.
42. Ibid., 62.
43. Ibid., 64.
44. Quoted in ibid., 66.
45. Church to Alexander, May 1, 1907, quoted in ibid., 66.
46. Ibid., 66.
47. Ibid., 69.
48. Ibid., 69.
49. This created a structure similar to what economic geographer Walter Christaller called "central place theory" — a model describing the location of different types of economic services and functions provided by cities relative to their population. See Walter Christaller, *Central Places in Southern Germany* (Englewood Cliffs, NJ: Prentice-Hall, 1966).
50. Davies (1976), 281.
51. Carstensen (1984), 80.
52. Ibid., 81.
53. Ibid., 80.
54. Davies (1976), 177.
55. Woodruff to New York, May 20, 1876, quoted in ibid., 177.
56. Ibid., 177.
57. Mitchell to London, April 20, 1888, quoted in ibid., 175.
58. Ibid., 176.
59. Quoted in ibid., 182.
60. Quoted in ibid., 185.
61. Ibid., 186.
62. Harold McCormick to Mr. W.S. Krebs, June 12, 1903. Wisconsin Historical Society, McCormick-International Harvester Collection.
63. Letter to B.A. Kennedy, June 6, 1905. Wisconsin Historical Society, McCormick-International Harvester Collection.
64. Ibid.
65. T.A. LaPorte to J.A. Chapman, May 25, 1905. Wisconsin Historical Society, McCormick-International Harvester Collection.
66. Ibid.
67. Ibid.
68. Carstensen (1984), 143.

69. John Chapman to George F. Steele, April 10, 1905. Wisconsin Historical Society, McCormick-International Harvester Collection.
70. Carstensen (1984), 161.
71. C.H. McCormick's Interviews Regarding Russian Factory, London Interview, 1909 (unpublished manuscript), Wisconsin Historical Society, McCormick-International Harvester Collection.
72. St. Petersburg Interviews (unpublished manuscript), Wisconsin Historical Society, McCormick-International Harvester Collection.
73. Ibid.
74. Carstensen (1984), 225–234.

3

The "Great Civilizer" and Equalizer: Gender, Race, and Civilization in Singer Advertising

If the visitor, standing within the largest building that has been erected by man, cast his eye upward ... he would see a chaste, beautiful and extensive inclosure that would at once invite him to ascend the broad staircase leading by easy stages to the scene of culture and civilization which awaited.
— "Singer Manufacturing Co. at the Exposition," *Halligan's Illustrated World's Fair*, 5 (October 1893), 672.

This is a fertile, well-watered country of South Africa, on the Indian Ocean, and forms a part of the region known as Kaffraria. The native Zulus are a fine warlike people of the Bantu stock, speaking the Bantu language. This language extends over more than half of Africa and is one of great beauty and flexibility. The Zulu bids fair to be as forward in civilization as he has been in war. Our group represents the Zulus after less than a century of civilization. Worth wins everywhere. Our agent at Cape Town supplies both the European and native inhabitants of Zululand, The Transvaal, and Free Orange State with thousands of Singer machines.
— Singer trade card, 1892.

A visit to Singer's pavilion inside the Manufacturers and Liberal Arts Building at the 1893 Columbian Exposition in Chicago was as much an educational as an entertaining affair. After entering at the ground level and viewing women demonstrating different sewing techniques on various Singer machines, one ascended the stairway and entered a model home, with rooms decorated in historical styles, complete with elaborate furnishings and architectural detailing. Signs pointed out that all the fabrics used in each room, including the tapestries and upholsteries, were made on Singer machines. On the first floor, visitors learned about the different styles of Singer machines available and what they could produce. On the second, they were given lessons about proper domesticity. Without even opening a book, women visitors to the exhibit could experience and see for themselves how to make a home into, as the first quote above suggests, a "scene of culture and civilization." To ensure these lessons were not forgotten, Singer made available trade cards depicting each of the historical tapestries that hung in the rooms. Women could take these cards home to study or to decorate their mantles or paste in their scrapbooks.

Other cards were available as well. On the way out of the exhibit downstairs, all visitors were given a set of 36 nation cards depicting the Singer machines in use around the world, with a verbal and visual description of each country. These cards were informative about civilization and culture, but in a way different from the tapestry cards, a way that positioned the Singer as, according to one company logo, the "Great Civilizer." The card depicting Zululand, for example, explained that Zulus are trying to be "forward in civilization." Similar, though not identical, messages were found on the other 35 cards. Like the historical tapestry cards, these giveaways could also be studied for lessons about culture or collected and hung on mantles as decorative pieces.

A quick "read" of these two sets of promotional strategies reveals much about Singer's advertising success. On the one hand, the tapestry trade cards associated the Singer Manufacturing Company with high culture — European history and style — suggesting a deferential role for American women in regard to their European sisters. On the other hand, the nation cards associated Singer with international civilizing efforts and suggested that American women served as models for women in the rest of the world. Both of these associations helped sell Singer machines by linking them to civilization. Women could produce on their machines artifacts that associated them and their families with the highest of culture, and while doing so, they were, figuratively at least, participating in another aspect of high culture — they were exemplars to other women of how to be civilized. A woman leaving the Singer pavilion at the Columbian Exposition, then, walked away feeling a major participant in civilizing efforts; sewing was an act that satisfied her desire to create a better home, thereby fulfilling her "proper" role within the civilized, patriarchal family *and* made her feel part of the civilizing process overseas.

These messages certainly weren't unique to Singer, nor were they invented only for the Columbian Exposition. However, they suggest how the Singer Manufacturing Company drew on the complex discourse of civilization to sell its products and, in so doing, how it created and reiterated a particular American view of the world, a geography of the world that situated each country along a temporal chain of progress. For Singer, whose primary consumers were women, that chain of progress was directly linked to notions of domesticity, femininity, and womanhood. This chapter explores the stories that Singer Company's advertisements told about civilization, progress, race, and gender. Singer's ads drew on the complex discourses of civilization and consumption to produce ads and other promotional devices that affirmed *and* deconstructed the superior status of the United States and of American women. At the same time, and related to this deconstruction, Singer's advertising also worked to reaffirm differences based on geography — that is, on regional and national boundaries. In other words, a close and contextual reading of Singer's advertising materials reveals a more complex view of the relationships between gender, race, class, and consumption than has been traditionally assigned to imperial cultural products such as advertising. My analysis focuses on two particular types of Singer advertising: the displays at the 1876 and 1893 expositions and the various series of trade cards the company produced and advertisements it ran in popular magazines throughout the last decades of the 19th and first decade of the 20th centuries.

Exhibiting Femininity

One of the keys to Singer's success as America's first large multinational company was its investment in advertising. The company took every opportunity to promote its products to large audiences and, in the second half of the 19th century, no one stage was any larger than what was offered at the international expositions. The Centennial Exhibition, held in Philadelphia in 1876 to commemorate the 100th anniversary of American independence, was the first such staging in the United States, and Singer invested heavily. The Centennial celebration of the nation's maturation to "manhood" was symbolized by the centerpiece of the Exposition — the Corliss engine, a giant block of steel and iron that ran ceaselessly and seemingly effortlessly in the center of the displays in Machinery Hall. It was *the* object of admiration, with contemporary images depicting visitors standing in awe of the oversized machine. A different sort of admiration occurred several hundred feet away, in the Singer Manufacturing Company's Sewing Machine Building. Singer was the only company to establish its own building for commercial display. If not exactly sublime in the sense of the Corliss engine, the sewing machines nonetheless elicited some strong emotions. As one contemporary guidebook described it, one of the rooms within the building contained "show-cases filled with dresses" that "were enough to drive an ordinary woman crazy."[1] The dresses, examples of what could be sewn on the machines, were just one of the temptations of this building. Visitors could sign the register, thereby entering their names in a contest to win the two-millionth manufactured Singer sewing machine. This made the Singer Building a very popular attraction among the women visitors to the Centennial. While not exactly countering the attractions of the Corliss, Singer's displays did bring the "machine" down to a much more manageable size, domesticating it and displaying it as a commodity to be consumed.

American-made machines of all sizes and uses were exhibited throughout the fairgrounds. Of the five primary buildings, two were explicitly devoted to mechanization — Machinery Hall and Agricultural Hall (agricultural implements). In addition, machines of all sorts were on display throughout other buildings, including the Singer building. In 1876, these technological wonders signified America's rise to industrial prominence, and some, like the sewing machine, were being mass-produced for sale overseas. But this overseas experience was hardly mentioned at the Exhibition. Singer, for example, with sales outside American borders well exceeding 40% of its total production,[2] made no mention of this fact in its advertisement, nor did most other sewing machine companies who were also engaged in international sales. What was on display at the Centennial, then, was the progress of an American economic "empire" that spread over national space, not international. These were machines for the nation.

The discourse of civilization provided the organizing schema for these displays of industry. As Robert Rydell points out, "The idea of progress made manifest at the Centennial International Exhibition of 1876, in short, was presented along racial lines in an organizational system devised by several eminent scientists."[3] Yet for companies like Singer, whose main appeal was to women, the language of gender, not race, was the primary focus of its displays. The Singer Building, for example, drew heavily on Victorian notions of bourgeois femininity to sell it products. Sewing had a long history in the United States as being a job for women done at home. And even though by 1876, factory use of sewing machines was becoming widespread, Singer targeted for its primary market machines for domestic use and made every effort to present itself as a company that supported women's proper role in the domestic sphere. In other words, Singer's advertising was all about associating the company and its products with the home and Victorian notions of feminine respectability, obscuring from view the sweat shops and other sites of production where a large percentage of sewing machines were being used by laboring women. Singer therefore paid special attention to the domestic aspects of their products, hiding their productive uses. For example, eschewing the display space that most other sewing machine companies used at the Fair — in a special section of Machinery Hall — Singer Company spent the extra money ($20,000 according to McCabe[4]) to build and staff their own building.

The building design itself spoke of upper-class femininity. As described by James McCabe in *The Illustrated History of the Centennial Exhibition*, it "is a pretty frame cottage ... handsomely frescoed within, and is fitted up in elegant style."[5] Another guidebook described the building as "handsome and elaborately fitted up ... one of the most attractive private exhibition buildings on the Centennial grounds. It is a Gothic structure, built on a raised eminence, and surrounded with grassy banks and flower-beds."[6] In other words, the Singer Building was designed to resemble an elegant residence. This "home" was divided into rooms: "a large and magnificent show-room, besides parlors, receptions-rooms, ladies' retiring-rooms, offices, etc., all of which are rich and elegantly furnished."[7] The building therefore presented a "safe" and feminine space for women at the Centennial — a place similar to their home where they could relax and socialize. In an advertisement for the building that appeared in many of the Centennial Exhibition guidebooks, Singer made explicit its association to femininity (see Figure 3.1). The ad describes the building as a "pretty home-like cottage style building located in one of the most picturesque spots of the Centennial grounds." Nearby, the ad is clear to point out, were other "feminine" spaces, such as the Pennsylvania Educational Building, the Restaurant Lafayette, Horticultural Hall, and the Music Pavilion. In contrast to the sublimity of the Corliss Engine located in the huge Machinery Hall, the Singer machines were in a cottage, located in the domesticated part of the fairgrounds.

Yet Singer's advertising relayed other messages too. In addition to its association with proper domesticity, Singer's ads spoke of a role for women beyond the home. For example, one of the company's gimmicks at the Exhibition was that it was giving away by lottery its two-millionth machine. This gimmick was proudly proclaimed in its advertisements and noted in most of the Exhibition guidebooks

THE SINGER MANUFACTURING CO'S SEWING MACHINE BUILDING.

THIS pretty home-like cottage style building is located in one of the most picturesque spots within the Centennial grounds, being on Landsdowne drive, almost directly back of Memorial Hall. Here also are located the Pennsylvania Educational Building, and the Restaurant Lafayette, on the same drive, a little to the west of this building. Across the Landsdowne Valley is Horticultural Hall, access to which is had from this point, by a new bridge crossing the valley. The grand Music Pavillion is placed not far from this bridge.

In interior arrangement, the Singer building is designed to display to advantage the machines and manufactures of the Company, the floor space being divided into a show room, a reception parlor and retiring rooms.

About twenty-five operatives will be constantly in attendance.

The Singer Manufacturing Company have on exhibition at their Centennial building, (Lansdowne drive, near Memorial Hall,) the (2,000,000) two-millionth machine of their manufacture.

This Machine it is proposed to present to some one of the visitors to their building, at the close of the Exhibition.

For this purpose a register of names will be kept, and the disposition will be determined by lot.

Go and see it!   You may be the fortunate one who will get it!

With fifteen active competing companies, the Singer Company has made and sold nearly half of all the sewing machines that have been produced for years. This fact speaks louder than premiums or medals, as it is the award of the common sense of the whole civilized world.

Principal Office, 34 Union Square, New York.   Philadelphia Office, 1106 Chestnut St.

Figure 3.1   Advertisement for the Singer Manufacturing Company's building at the 1876 Centennial Exhibition. (The Historical Society of Pennsylvania, Philadelphia)

— visible proof of the long-term productivity of the company. The ad mentioned above ends with the following lines: "With fifteen active competing companies, the Singer Company has made and sold nearly half of all the sewing machines that have been produced for years. This fact speaks louder than premiums or medals, as it is the award of the common sense of the whole civilized world." So too, on a trade card for Singer given out at the Fair, the company, under the title "The Singer Still Triumphant!" lists its sales numbers compared to its competitors (Singer sold 249,852 machines in 1875; the next on the list was the Wheeler and Wilson Company, which sold 103,740 machines). Women therefore were being enticed to buy the machines not only because of their association to proper femininity but also because the purchase made them participants in the "common sense of the whole civilized world" — that is, participants in modernity and progress and members of the "civilized" race. As we shall see, this double message (civilization at home through proper domesticity and civilization beyond through the "civilizing" effects of sewing) was an enduring feature of the company's promotional campaigns, and Singer used its international status to refine and strengthen it in later years.

This double message is also clear from an examination of Singer's displays at the 1893 Columbian Exposition held in Chicago. Unlike the 1876 Centennial, Singer did not erect its own building, but instead exhibited its machines in four different displays within three different buildings. They chose this manner of display because, as a contemporary article commented, the company had asked for an amount of space equaling one twenty-fifth of the entire amount within the main building, the Manufactures and Liberal Arts Building, and the authorities were unable to accommodate this demand.[8] Like Singer's "home" at the Centennial Exhibition, Singer constructed all their displays in forms that were considered appropriately "feminine," particularly the two-story pavilion they built within the massive main exhibit hall. The two floors served as an important divider for the exhibit. On the first floor were two large rooms that contained 10 young women demonstrating the various uses of the different types of sewing machines manufactured by Singer, as well as "sofas and chairs for the weary visitor."[9] This location is also where the nation trade cards were given out, depicting women and men in other countries using Singer machines. Ascending the main staircase, the visitor entered a sort of model home, complete with reception hall, bedroom, and dining room, all of which were elaborately decorated (as the exhibit brochure mentioned, the floors of the reception hall were made of San Domingo mahogany, the walls were ivory, and the ceiling relief work was cream and gold), and draped with materials — curtains, bedspreads, cushions, upholstery, and art prints — that had been made on Singer machines. And, as the Singer brochure pointed out, "on the entire floor no Sewing Machine is seen."[10] In other words, Singer clearly divided their overtly commercial display from their cultural, domestic display. The rooms of the model home were meant to "please the eye and elevate and educate the taste";[11] they were didactic spaces, therefore, meant as domestic object lessons for women. The "modern bedchamber" was described as a "perfect study in color harmony," whereas the Henry VIII dining room was "historically correct in every thing, save the electric lighting."[12] Women visitors then could learn about the latest in modern home design, including historic revival styles, without even entering the Woman's Building at the Exposition, where specific exhibits about the emerging profession of interior design were on view. Singer brought domestic displays representing the highest ideals of civilized womanhood right into the heart of the Manufactures and Liberal Arts Building. *Halligan's Illustrated World's Fair* described it thus: "If the visitor, standing within the largest building that has been erected by man, cast his eye upward ... he would see a chaste, beautiful and extensive inclosure that would at once invite him to ascend the broad staircase leading by easy stages to the scene of culture and civilization which awaited."[13]

Although less grandiose, the other three Singer displays were similar in their attempts to associate sewing machines with high culture. In the Palace of Mechanic Arts, also called Machinery Hall, Singer constructed a pavilion with an ornate white and gold exterior. *Halligan's Illustrated World's Fair* noted its similarity to the pavilion in the Manufactures and Liberal Arts Building: "Here is the same delicacy of architectural treatment, from wainscoting to balustrade; the garlanded frieze and paneled roof ornaments offering especially fine effects, all in keeping with the exquisite art of the modern seamstress."[14] Inside the pavilion was a large room decorated with similar attention to detail, housing women demonstrating the various machines (194 of them!) that Singer produced for industrial use. Singer's pavilion in the Shoe and Leather Building followed a parallel design — decorative exterior (white and gold) and interior finishes, this time containing displays of the machines for use in leather industries. *Halligan's* described the display as "the finest thing of the kind in the Shoe and Leather building, and sustained the character and good fame of Singer architecture elsewhere in the park."[15] Even though the potential customers that Singer hoped to attract in these displays of machines for industrial use were men, the company still needed to maintain its association with civilized womanhood through its role as the purveyor of beauty and culture.

These displays were also about proclaiming the "character and good fame of Singer architecture"[16] around the world. In the Machinery Hall pavilion, for example, were not only displays of machines but also cases filled with the manufactured products made on such machines in different parts of the world — good advertisements, commentators noted, for the extent of the Singer empire: "It is doubtful if any better advertisement of the vast extent of the Singer company's business could have been made than this showing of goods manufactured in all quarters of the globe."[17] Singer's first sentence in its brochure for its display in the Manufactures and Liberal Arts Building explains that they put together such elegant exhibits "out of a desire to put its machines before the assembled nations, in a manner befitting its world-wide reputation."[18]

Singer also used its worldwide reputation to explicitly promote sales. As previously mentioned, in addition to the tapestry cards, all visitors to Singer's primary exhibit were given a box containing 36 lithographed cards "representing the costumes of different countries."[19] The nation cards proved to be one of Singer's most successful advertising schemas and were reprinted and augmented throughout the first decades of the 20th century. The tapestry cards disappeared after the Exposition. Singer, in other words, found that associating their products with one aspect of the discourse of civilization — where women were active in bringing proper domesticity to "others" — was more effective as an advertising tool than the association to civilization in the form of high culture at home. Let me turn then to an analysis of these nation cards, in order to understand in what ways they "worked" as advertisements and as forms of geographical knowledge.

The United Nations of Singer

As described in chapter 2, Singer was a successful international company as early as the mid-19th century, selling a majority of its machines outside of American borders by 1879. It is within the context of these foreign experiences that Singer developed one of its most successful promotional strategies — a set of trade cards that depicted people from these countries dressed in "native" clothing using Singer machines. Originally issued in 1892, these nation cards proved so popular that the company added to its original 36 cards and developed several more sets that were printed well into the first decade of the 20th century. Although not Singer's sole source of advertising (the company avidly invested in advertisements and was particularly keen on producing trade card sets), the nation cards series was considered by the company one of its most popular and successful forms of advertising.[20] Because each card contained on it a verbal description of the country or region depicted, these advertising sets formed a type of geographical gazetteer of the world, providing information and interesting images of people and clothing that were meant to be both entertaining and informative. Like other aspects of Singer's promotional strategies, these cards were in part didactic — that is, tools for learning.

All of the cards followed a similar visual and verbal format (see Figure 3.2 and Figures 3.4 to 3.8). On the front of each card was a color lithograph depicting "native" peoples dressed in "native" clothing posed around the Singer machine, with one person actually operating the machine. The name of the country or, at times, the city or region, was printed to one side. The flip side of the card contained a written description of that place, most often beginning with a description of its location and physical geographic characteristics and then moving into the culture of the people, their "race," customs, clothing, character, language, and history. This description ended with a statement about the Singer machine's use in that particular place or its success in "civilizing" the people of the region. The places depicted all represented parts of the world where Singer was present, either by operating its own stores or having machines sold through general merchants. The majority of the cards from 1892 to 1894 depicted places in Western and Eastern Europe, but they were not limited to those countries. Other places depicted included Zululand, Ceylon, India, Manila, China, Japan, and Burma.

Exactly how decisions were made about the places depicted on these cards is difficult to determine. Singer executives obviously chose places that they thought would attract the attention of middle-class American women — some because of the exoticness of the place, some because of the unusual dress. Each card was a mini geography lesson, but one with overtly commercial goals. These lessons were relayed both through the image and through the written descriptions. In general, two types of images were used: one that the depicted the Singer machines in use in an actual home setting, showing details of that home, and another that used a fairly generic background that gave few details of its space. Most of the first set — those printed in 1892 — used a generic background that lent a more standardized look to each card.

Let me focus briefly on six cards (Zululand, Ceylon, Spain, Roumania, India, and Japan) to give some sense of the range of geographical knowledges offered by Singer in this first set. These cards

Figure 3.2   Singer trade card of Zululand, 1892. (Collection of the author)

are fairly representative of the group and depict a range of countries (European, African, and Asian) and situations (colonized and colonizers, black and white). In the 1890s, geography lessons at American schools would have sorted these countries into a strict hierarchy of civilization based on race, degree of gender specialization, and stage of economic growth. This discourse of civilization was certainly evident in these Singer trade cards, both in their visual and verbal descriptions, but the messages relayed therein were more complicated and at times contradictory than the hierarchy of civilization would normally allow. For example, an analysis of the images alone suggests that Roumania and India are lower in the civilizational "family of man" because these cards depict men using the Singer machine, indicating that clear lines of gender specialization had not been attained. In late 19th century America, sewing was most definitely a woman's job, and all other sewing machine advertisement of the time showed a white, middle-class woman using the machine. The Zululand card is particularly interesting because it portrays a quintessential, patriarchal family posing around the Singer: a father figure to the left, shown in a pose that expresses patriarchal power (with hat and cane), a mother actively using the machine, and others, including children, looking on. Visually, it is similar to the cards of Spain and Ceylon. The images work to sort these countries into an organizational frame, but one that complicates the racial lines of civilization, situating Zululand higher on the civilization ladder than Roumania.

The image of Zululand is also of interest because its depiction of black bodies is so different from depictions of African-American bodies within American advertising. It is almost impossible to find images of African Americans that depict them in a setting that accords them respect. As many scholars have shown,[21] for the most part, black bodies in American advertising were used as gimmicks, or sidekicks, to sell products. African Americans themselves were never depicted as the actual consumers of goods but were rather imagined as decorative devices, there to attract attention. In a similar way, within the British context, African bodies were also used as attention-getters, never as the potential users of consumer products. According to Anne McClintock, the presentation of raced bodies in British Victorian ads, like the use of white idealized figures of women, was strictly for illustrative and decorative purposes or, as she says, they are "figured not as historic agents but as frames for the commodity, valued for *exhibition* alone" (emphasis in original).[22] In these ads, the commodity itself becomes the agent of historical change, doing the "civilizing work of empire."[23] For example, in "the birth of civilization" ad for Pear's Soap (see Figure 3.3), the soap itself transforms, at the moment of contact, the "savage" black man into a civilized consumer. Further, the man is feminized through his decorative feathers and by the portrayal of his body as the object of visual consumption. As McClintock argues, "in advertising scenes set in the colonies, African men are *feminized* and portrayed as exhibition frames for commodity display."[24]

The Singer card of Zululand presents a different version of raced bodies. As a Western, modern commodity, the Singer machine certainly is presented as an active agent of change, doing, in the words of McClintock, the "civilizing work of empire"[25] and thereby reinforcing racism based on hierarchical notions of civilization. Yet the people on the card are individuated, not idealized; they are presented posed and facing the viewer head-on. Instead of the commodity "abstracted from social context and human labor"[26] doing the active work of civilization alone, the Zululand card depicts people using the machine and producing clothing, just as white women are presented using sewing machines in a wide range of advertising images that circulated at the time. In other words, these foreigners are presented as historical actors, as agents of their own transformation, not simply as "frames for the commodity,"[27] as McClintock suggests. In fact, as suggested earlier, the people of Zululand are depicted as the prototypical patriarchal family, with male head of household surrounded by his wife and children. The man certainly is not feminized and his body is not portrayed as an object of visual consumption.

Figure 3.3 "The Birth of Civilization," Pears' soap advertisement. (Anne McClintock, *Imperial Leather: Race, Gender and Sexuality in the Colonial Conquest* [New York: Routledge, 1995], 224.)

A reading of the visual portions of these trade cards, therefore, offers a more complicated schema of the hierarchy of nations than one would expect from reading contemporary geography textbooks or advertising materials within the British context. The verbal descriptions on the back of these cards add another layer of information and complication. Let me start with the description of Zululand that was printed on the back of the card:

This is a fertile, well-watered country of South Africa, on the Indian Ocean, and forms a part of the region known as Kaffraria. The native Zulus are a fine warlike people of the Bantu stock, speaking the Bantu language. This language extends over more than half of Africa and is one of great

Figure 3.4   Singer trade card of Ceylon, 1892. (Collection of the author)

beauty and flexibility. The Zulu bids fair to be as forward in civilization as he has been in war. Our group represents the Zulus after less than a century of civilization. Worth wins everywhere. Our agent at Cape Town supplies both the European and native inhabitants of Zululand, The Transvaal, and Free Orange State with thousands of Singer machines.

Implied in this text and image is that the use of Singer machines can make people "white." As portrayed on the card, the people of Zululand are not quite there yet — they are barefoot and are not adorned with decorative clothing — but presumably with more sewing and machinery, the Zulus would be as "forward in civilization as ... in war."[28]

Two other cards depicted family-type situations as well: Ceylon and Spain. On the flip side of the Ceylon card was written:

This is a picturesque island in the Indian Ocean, separated from Peninsular India by the Gulf of Manaar. It is 271 miles long by 137 wide, is a Crown colony of Great Britain and entirely independent of British India. Its capital city is Colombo. The dominant race is the Singhalese, who are genuine Buddhists and very tenacious of their castes. There are also many natives of Arabic descent, besides the Portugese, Dutch and English. Our photo, taken on the spot, represents the Singer Manufacturing Company's employees in their national costume. The Company have offices in all the principal cities, and sell a large number of machines.

Most of the text, like on the card for Zululand, is taken up with a description of the country (location, race, religion, language) in a manner similar to a gazetteer. No direct mention is made of the civilizing work of the Singer Company per se, but the image suggests the connections between proper notions of domesticity and the use of the sewing machine. The image presents the two people as a couple, with the patriarch standing over his presumed wife as she works on the machine, and the setting is decorated with an elaborate carpet. Yet the text makes clear that these two are employees, bound together by work and not necessarily marriage. Singer mentioned this fact on several of its cards, alerting the reader to the nativeness of the company's employees as well as its consumers. This "fact" disrupts several assumptions about imperial relationships and representations. First, it makes clear that "others" (even "other" women) were important to Singer not only as consumers, but as salespeople — those dispensing the "great civilizer." But perhaps more importantly, it presents these "others" as active agents in their own representations. By stating that the image depicts "employees in their national costume," the text suggests that they are dressing up, posing for the viewer, playing "native." So too, they are playing at being the patriarchal couple. They are, in fact, Ceylonese employees of Singer, dressed up as natives performing the roles of patriarchal husband and wife. This positions these people as agents in their own representation, playing a role for the viewers.

The description on the back of the Spain card provides more detailed information about physical geography and does not specify "race" as a category. The description is titled "Corunna":

This is the Northernmost Province of Spain, a part of the old Province of Galicia, bounded North and West by the Sea. The country is very mountainous, craggy and picturesque, and essentially agricultural. The inhabitants are descendants of the ancient Goths. They are not very tall, but stout and robust. Corunna, the capital, was founded by the Phoenicians several centuries B.C. Our picture represents the Provincial dress of the rural population, in a multitude of whose homes you will find our Grand Old "Singer."

Again, this card makes no direct reference to the civilizing work of the Singer. However, this region of Spain is described in very quaint

$PAIN.

COPYRIGHT 1892 BY THE SINGER MANUFACTURING CO   OVER

Figure 3.5   Singer trade card of Spain, 1892. (Collection of the author)

terms (the landscape is "picturesque", the people "stout and robust") and is noted to be primarily agricultural and, thus, not entirely civilized. This description resembles that offered on the back of the Roumania card:

> A kingdom of Southern Europe, comprising the old Principalities of Moldavia, Wallachia and Dobrudja. It is bounded East and North by the Pruth, South by the Danube, West and North-west by the Carpathian Mountains. It is mountainous in the West, but level toward the East. The climate is subject to extremes of cold and heat. Large numbers of Horses, Sheep and Cattle are raised, also Grains in abundance. The first authentic inhabitants were the Daciens, who were conquered

ROUMANIA.

COPYRIGHT 1892 BY THE SINGER MANUFACTURING CO   OVER

Figure 3.6 Singer trade card of Roumania, 1892. (Collection of the author)

and the country colonized by the Romans. The Roumania of to-day is a mixture of the Indo-Caucasian and Mongrol races. They are good looking, intelligent and fairly energetic. The national dress is rich in embroidery and lacings. These are typical Roumanians; their rich brunette complexion enhanced by their highly colored dress. The Singer Company have several offices here and sell numbers of machines.

Attention is paid to the history of the country and to the physical appearance of the people — all in a tone that highlights their traditional, not yet completely modern, culture.

Though resembling in visual form that of Roumania, the card of India offers a striking contrast in verbal description:

An extensive Empire of the British Crown, consisted of the Great Southern Peninsula of Southern Asia, and a narrow strip along the East side of the Bay of Bengal. It is bounded

INDIA

COPYRIGHT 1892 BY THE SINGER MANUFACTURING CO.   OVER

Figure 3.7 Singer trade card of India, 1892. (Collection of the author)

North by the Himalaya Mountains, West by a Mountain Range, East by parallel offshoots from the opposite extremity of the Himalayas, and on the other side by the Indian Ocean. The surface of the country is extremely diversified. It has the highest mountain peak (Mt. Everest) in the world, the Ganges River — wonderful for its annual inundations of the immense Gangetic Plain. There is great diversity of race and language; in Upper India the inhabitants are of the Indo-European stock, with a language allied in the roots to the Sanscrit. The religions are Mohammedanism and Brahmanism. The aboriginal races have no literature. The governing races are of Arabic, Brahmanical and Persian stock. Under

British rule India is making rapid strides in modern civilization. Our picture represents the Singer Manufacturing Company's native employees in their usual costume. The Singer Sewing Machines has been a factor in helping the people of India toward a better civilization for nearly twenty years, and thousands of them are in use.

This description is certainly one of the longest offered on the set of cards, understandable given the vastness and diversity of the country. Of particular interest here is the rather striking reference to the "aboriginal races" as having "no literature," and the alignment of the Singer machine with British rule in bringing "civilization" to India, an explicit example of how colonial and commercial imperialism were discursively joined. The fact that the people depicted on the card are Singer employees may help to explain why they are men; Singer archives suggest that they rarely if ever were able to hire Indian women, who for religious and social reasons were prevented from working in situations where they would come into contact with men not from their family.

Perhaps the most curious of the six cards is that of Japan. The image shows a woman dressed in "native" clothes who is sewing a clearly Western-styled men's jacket. If one saw a similar image today, the typical assumption would be that it depicts a woman worker in a sweatshop, toiling for low wages to produce clothing cheaply for Western manufacturers. In 1892, the situation was less clear. Here is the descriptor on the back:

An insular empire of Asia, composed of 3,850 Islands, the principal of which are Hando and Kio Siu. The capital city of Tokio is on the Island of Hando at the head of the Bay of Yedo. The inhabitants are of the Mongolian race, are stout and well formed, amiable, intelligent and patriotic. The state religion has always been Sintoism. The priests are supposed to have descended from the Sun. Japan has a written history for more than twenty-five centuries, and a continuous dynasty since 660 B.C. This picture was taken on the spot and is an exact representation of the native costume. The Singer Manufacturing Co. have offices in all the ports and large cities, and are furnishing the Japanese with thousands of Singer Machines.

No mention is made of the Western jacket, only indirectly in its contrast to the "exact representation of the native costume." What is

Figure 3.8   Singer trade card of Japan, 1892. (Collection of the author)

highlighted here is Japan's long history as a cohesive culture — the reference to the length of its written history, the fact of its long-standing dynasty, the reference to its people as "patriotic." As Susan Schulten suggests, Japan figured prominently in the American geographical imagination in the late 19th and early 20th centuries; it was a fascination because of its long-standing and somewhat "civilized" culture that had remained hidden from the Euro-American gaze for so long.[29] Its culture was both admired and treated with suspicion. This trade card expresses this ambivalence. First, the woman is clearly sewing not for her own domestic use, but for export, as a commodity. She was involved, in other words, in manufacturing, an economic "stage" given high regard in the civilizational hierarchy, yet one not suitable for a proper "white" woman. Her culture is described with respect, yet her religion with suspicion.

My reading of this sample of six cards suggests the complexity of messages they contained and conveyed. These cards were certainly of their time and place, in the sense that they provided information and relayed images similar to what was being presented elsewhere at the 1893 Columbian Exposition. For example, these cards fulfilled an educational purpose, providing visual and textual information about "others" around the world, similar to the range of exhibits offered within many of the Exposition's sites, where, as Henry Adams wrote "education ran riot."[30] This was particularly apparent in the anthropological displays, where the "lessons" of evolution were taught. For example, one of the most popular of these displays included "living" exhibits of native peoples. With the help of Indian agents, Frederick Putnam, the anthropologist in charge, persuaded Indians from an array of tribes to come to Chicago and participate in living displays depicting their traditional ways of life.[31] Apparently some of the participating Indians had to be taught by anthropologists about these "traditional" ways, because they were a generation or two removed from that knowledge. Several years after the Exposition, a head of the Carlisle Indian School reflected: "In some cases the ethnologists who managed had to show the Indians how to build and dress because none of the present generation in such tribes knew."[32] So too, even the overtly commercial and entertainment-oriented displays along the midway section of the Exposition "educated" the public about "other" cultures, with living displays of "exotic" peoples from around the world, all dressed in their "native" clothes. In the case of Native Americans, this provided object lessons about the stages of humankind's "savage" past, whereas the displays of, for example, the Dahomey peoples on the Midway suggested that savagery still existed in spatially remote regions of the world.

Singer's nation cards similarly depicted peoples in their "native" clothes, not in modern Western clothes, thereby providing depictions of the less-than-civilized state of contemporary cultures around the world. In this way, these cards reflect a view of the world very much in accord with the dominant scientific ideas of racism and evolution that prevailed in fields of anthropology, ethnology, and geography. On the other hand, because many of these cards represented raced peoples as active agents in their own civilizing process — either through visual clues that represented raced bodies as individual subjects or through textual clues that suggested the active agency of the figures in their own representation — the Singer nation cards express alternative ways of understanding and seeing "otherness."

Figure 3.9   Singer trade card of Lerwick, 1894. (Collection of the author)

It is important to recognize that Singer limited its representations of "otherness" to those living outside the boundaries of the United States. In fact, I suggest that although the nation cards erased some forms of difference, they actively worked to reassert other forms of difference, in this case, geographical difference. Every one of these trade cards constructs national or regional difference from the United States. This work is done through the image, particularly through the depiction of "native" costume and, of course, in the textual material on the back that, as previously mentioned before, reads like a geographical gazetteer.

This inscribing of geographical difference became even more evident when Singer released additional cards in 1894. In this new series, Singer added "native" dwellings and interior decoration to the depiction of geographical difference. In other words, these cards showed people using Singer machines in their "native" homes, dressed in their "native" clothes. For example, the card of Lerwick (see Figure 3.9) portrays regional character by showing the inside of a crofter's cottage, with women engaged in both the old and new ways of textile production — a sewing machine and a spinning wheel. The text on the back contains detailed information that describes the exact location of Lerwick and its history, followed by this:

> This picture represents the interior of a crofter's cottage in Shetland. The crofters earn their livelihood by cultivating the small holdings which they rent; and in the case of the coast towns, by fishing also. The shawl worn by the old lady (the fisherman's mother), is a form of knit-work peculiar to

Figure 3.10   Singer trade card of Archangel, 1894. (Collection of the author)

the Shetland Islands, and valued very much on account of its softness and for its comfort.

This detailed description reads very much like an early 20th century folklore or cultural geography textbook, a way of cataloging different folk cultures around the world. The card labeled "Archangel" (see Figure 3.10) shows a family dressed in local clothing in front of their home — a one-room dwelling made of animal skin. On this card, the text gives a lengthy geographical and historical description of this Russian seaport town on the White Sea — the "chief commercial city for the North of Russia and Siberia" — and ends thus: "Lapps, Finns and Samoyeds (many of them still heathen) form the native population, but the larger part of the inhabitants are Russians. The picture shows a Samoyed family in their home or hut of skin — one of the women being at work sewing on a 'Singer' machine." This card then both deconstructs difference in the sense that these "heathens" are posed in a way to suggest a patriarchal family — therefore on their way to becoming "civilized" — and yet reinforces locational difference, particularly through the image of the dwelling, its rather barren setting, and the family's clothing.

These cards then combined the old with the new, the modern with the folk, without any apparent negative or disruptive effects. They conveyed that foreign people are both similar to white, middle-class Americans (living in patriarchal social settings, using Singer machines) and yet very different from them (inhabiting unusual house forms, dressing in exotic clothing, still participants in local folkways). This combination of the modern and the folk is apparent in the advertisements of other international companies as well. From the 1880s on, McCormick Harvesting Machine Company included images of foreigners using their machines in other countries, thus figuring them as modern; yet, these foreigners were always identified as non-Americans verbally through textual references and visually through their clothing (see Figures 4.28 and 4.30). A common motif of Kodak advertising in the first decades of the 20th century was to depict foreign peoples using their cameras dressed in stereotypical, "native" clothing and posed in places that are marked as foreign. For example, the windmill in Figure 3.11 clearly suggests the setting as the Netherlands, with the foreigners dressed in stereotypical Dutch fashion.

Singer made this merging of the modern and the folk one of its dominant advertising motifs. The sense of both familiarity and dissimilarity with foreign cultures is evident in a later set of nation cards that date from the turn of the century. In this set of cards, the weight of geographical description was carried by the image alone, and the back side of the cards contained uniform machine advertisements. The card of Sweden, for example (see Figure 3.12), is similar to the one of Lerwick: a patriarchal family is posed inside their home around a hearth, and both modern (Singer) and traditional (spinning wheel) forms of sewing are illustrated. The Sweden image is fuller, however, and more detailed in its depiction of building material, furniture, and household accoutrements. The card of Ecuador (see Figure 3.13) is an interesting comparison to Archangel — both with patriarchal families posed outside their homes, with a woman using the Singer machine. The details included in the Ecuador card include depictions of local flora and fauna and also hints about the nature of this family. Posted on the left side of the hut is a Singer sign, suggesting that this dwelling also serves as a Singer office, or at least as the home of a Singer employee. Singer's logo posted onto a traditional thatched hut encapsulates the message that the modern and the traditional can coexist. For American women collecting these cards, the message was that Singer machines were good because they worked to make foreign peoples civilized and therefore more similar to themselves, but not *completely* similar— these foreign peoples remained foreign, outside American culture. In other words, the commonality that American women could feel with their "sisters" abroad through their common consumption and use of Singer sewing machines was always undercut by, and made less threatening through, the maintenance of categories of dissimilarity.

If it isn't an Eastman, it isn't a Kodak.

Drawn for Eastman Kodak Co., by Edward Penfield.

Bring your Vacation Home in a

KODAK

Add to the after-delights of your holiday with pictures of
the people, the places and the sports you are interested
in. Every step easy by the Kodak System.

Kodaks, $5.00 to $108.00.   Brownies, $1.00 to $9.00.

EASTMAN KODAK CO.

*Catalogs at the
dealers or by mail*   Rochester, N. Y.

Figure 3.11   "Bring your Vacation Home in a Kodak," Kodak advertisement from *Harper's Magazine*, 1904. (Collection of the author)

The Sisterhood of Singer

At the same time that these different sets of nation cards were circulating through the United States, Singer developed other successful advertising schemes that drew on its international experiences. Singer combined its appeal to internationalism and modernity in a series of advertisements printed in popular magazines in the late 19th and early 20th centuries. In this series of ads, Singer aligned itself and its products with the "progress" of American women — positioning them as educated, modern, and somewhat independent — and used this as a measure of social "progress" for other cultures and other times. Moving away from any explicit association to the processes of civilization per se, these ads instead mentioned how the use of sewing machines had helped American women achieve their high standing. In these

Figure 3.12   Singer trade card of Sweden, circa 1900. (Collection of the author)

Figure 3.13   Singer trade card of Ecuador, circa 1900. (Collection of the author)

ads, Singer targets its advertising directly at women and women's issues, moving away from its earlier emphasis on bringing "civilization" to other cultures. Two series of ads ran concurrently and their messages reinforced each other.

In 1900, Singer printed a series of advertisements entitled "The Woman's Century: 1800–1900." Each of the ads in this series depicted, through words and images, the achievements and "progress" that American women had achieved throughout the 19th century. Figure 3.14, for example, appeared in *McClure's Magazine* in 1900. The center image portrays a woman in a traditional pose, sitting in her parlor using a Singer; the two images on the right show "modern" women — one dressed in her golfing gear, the other presumably engaged in some nondomestic work. These two images from 1900 are contrasted to images on the left of women in 1800. "Recreation in 1800" was apparently limited to embroidery, whereas "The Busy Woman of 1800" was engaged in the kitchen. The text makes clear the message: "In no country in the world is the diffusion of well being so general as among the women of the United States; this is largely due to their ready use of mechanical, labor-saving contrivances. It is in the invention of such machinery that American ingenuity excels; and the Singer sewing machine is one of its most conspicuous examples. For half-a-century it has been a most potent factor in promoting the happiness of women." To measure progress by the "state" of women is certainly not a new technique, nor was the Singer Manufacturing Company the only one to adopt it, but this ad represents something new for Singer, with its specific emphasis on the "progress" of women through time.

This direct temporal comparison was also used in an 1897 ad (see Figure 3.15) that contrasted the sewing activities of the feudal age with contemporary sewing techniques: "Stitching and embroidery were the chief accomplishments of ladies in the Feudal Age. Singer's inventions, and their development by his successors, have since made the art of sewing common to all. That the value of the sewing machine as a means of refinement is exceeded by the printing press may be an open question — but no question exists as to the superior excellence of Singer Machines for family sewing." In this advertisement, contrast is constituted through class — in feudal times, only some women were able to be "proper" women and conduct stitching activities, whereas sewing was now "common to all," and with it came "refinement."

At the same time as these temporal contrasts were presented in ads, Singer also continued its advertising schemes that focused on spatial contrasts. Using similar images to what appeared on their nation cards, Singer began an advertising campaign in popular magazines titled "Singer National Costume Series." This series portrayed women in "native" costumes using Singer machines, accompanied by a rather lengthy textual description (see Figures 3.16 to 3.20). An 1898

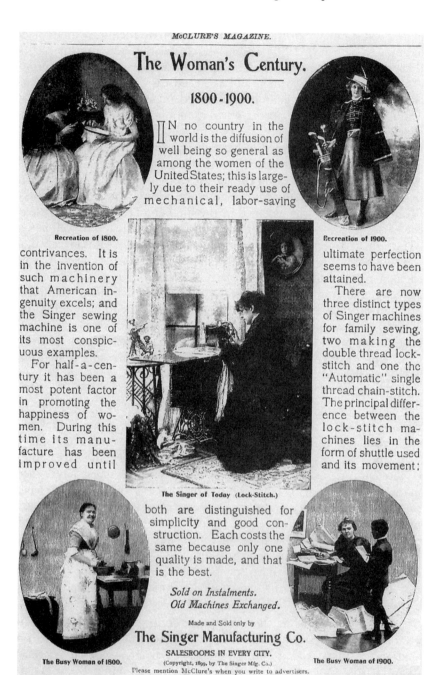

Figure 3.14 "The Woman's Century: 1800–1900," Singer advertisement from *McClure's Magazine,* 1900. (Collection of the author)

HOUSE FURNISHINGS 32

TITCHING AND EMBROIDERY

were the chief accomplishments of ladies in the Feudal Age. Singer's inventions, and their development by his successors, have since made the art of sewing common to all. That the value of the sewing machine as **a means of refinement** is exceeded by the printing press, may be an open question—but no question exists as to the superior excellence of

Singer Machines
————For Family Sewing————

Your choice of Three Distinct Types.

The Singer No. 15

Double Lock-Stitch.
Oscillating Shuttle.

The Dressmaker's Machine; especially adapted for high-speed operation, producing greatest quantity of fine stitching, and requiring least effort by the operator. Has unusually large bobbin for lower thread and finest mechanical adjustment. Greatest range of work and lightest-running lock-stitch machine in the world.

The Singer No. 24

Automatic
Chain-Stitch.

Guaranteed to be in every point the best single-thread chain-stitch machine on the market. The general advantages of this type of machine for family sewing comprise greatest ease and quietness of operation, simplicity of construction and elasticity of seam.

The Singer No. 27

Double Lock-Stitch.
Vibrating Shuttle.

More generally used for family sewing throughout the world than all other machines combined. The movement of the self-threading vibrating shuttle being shorter than in any other similar machine, less effort is required for its operation.

Made and sold only by **THE SINGER MANUFACTURING CO.** Offices in every city in the world.

Figure 3.15   "Accomplishments of Ladies in the Feudal Age," Singer advertisement from *Munsey's Magazine*, 1897. (Collection of the author)

ad called "The 'Dalkullan'" was the first to appear, and in it, Singer explained the series: "The accompanying illustration is reproduced from a photograph by our agent at Stockholm, Sweden, and is the first of a series of similar subjects obtained by us in like manner to illustrate national costumes all over the world." The rest of the text provides a description of the costumes worn by the Dalkullan — people native to Dalarne, an interior part of Sweden — ending with an accounting of the large amount of machines sold in Sweden. Like the set of nation cards, this series of ads exploited late 19th century anthropological interest in other races and cultures and associated that interest with a product of the Singer — clothing. But unlike those trade cards, these ads focused on providing information about women.

This focus becomes more clear in other advertisements that make direct reference to the plight of women in other countries. For example, the China ad included the following paragraph: "No respect is paid to women, the birth of a daughter being considered a misfortune. The average Chinese girl has no education, but is a slave to her family until, without any regard for her own wishes, a husband is chosen, when she must devote herself to his people." China, therefore, is being presented as less than modern, as "unprogressive," based on

SINGER NATIONAL COSTUME SERIES.

The "Dalkullan."

THE accompanying illustration is reproduced from a photograph by our agent at Stockholm, Sweden, and is the first of a series of similar subjects obtained by us in like manner to illustrate national costumes all over the world.

The characteristic tall blonde of the northern races is typified in this instance by a "Dalkullan," or native of Dalarne, a mountainous interior district of Sweden, where the old fashions and costumes are still preserved.

The two great silver buttons fastening the flowing collar, the brooches at the throat and bow, the belt clasp and other jewelry are silver heirlooms; the apron is homespun, in brilliant colors, similar to a Roman scarf. Sweden has given to us Jenny Lind, Neilson and other sweet singers. We send annually to her many thousand "American Singers," silent but useful.

THE SINGER MANUFACTURING CO.,
Offices all over the world.

Figure 3.16   Singer National Costume Series, "The Dalkullan," Singer advertisement, 1898. (Collection of the author)

SINGER
National Costume Series

THE IRISH PEASANT.

READERS of "Handy Andy" all know the merry, rollicking, good-hearted Irish lad whose counterpart is shown, pipe in hand, beside a sweet-faced Irish lass. These two, dressed in ordinary costume, were photographed in Londonderry, a seaport city of Northern Ireland, in the vicinity of which many typical Irish peasants are found who are still speaking the Celtic language.

The photograph represents the pair at a "Singer Sewing Machine." This has long been adopted as being the best for the national schools of Ireland, where its proper use forms one of the special subjects of instruction.

THE SINGER MANUFACTURING CO. OFFICES ALL OVER THE WORLD.

Figure 3.17   Singer National Costume Series, "The Irish Peasant," Singer advertisement from *The Outlook*, 1898. (Collection of the author)

SINGER
NATIONAL COSTUME
SERIES

THE SPANISH WOMAN.

IT has been said that every native Spanish woman is energetic; whether she be from Andalusia or Asturias, the south or of the north, she has none of the creole languor of the Spanish-descended woman of Cuba, Mexico and tropical America.

There is vim and force in the native Spaniard, and she is usually a better type than the man of her race. Our artist has sent to us five photos, showing distinct types of Spanish women: the Basque from the Pyrenees, the industrious Catalonian, a blue-eyed blonde from Salamanca, a stout Andalusian of the provincial class, a patriotic Galician from Corunna, and the one whom we present from old Seville together with her lover.

How characteristic are the accessories! The woman is industrious, and regards with an air of distinct disapproval the weak-faced individual before her with his guitar and glass of wine.

Many a Spanish woman would now be driven to hard straits were it not for the Singer sewing machine, which is furnished to her on the most liberal terms of payment; thus she easily becomes self-supporting.

Singer machines are almost universally used in Spain, because of their simplicity, great range of work and superior construction. They are "built like a watch," and never bother their fair operators, whether in Spain or elsewhere.

THE SINGER MFG. COMPANY.
Offices in every city in the world.

Figure 3.18   Singer National Costume Series, "The Spanish Woman," Singer advertisement from *The Outlook,* 1898. (Collection of the author)

SINGER National Costume Series.

CHINA.

OF all nations the Chinese are the most remarkable and eccentric, having, through nearly 5,000 years, retained one form of government, an unchanged language, and one religion—Tauism.

Because of governmental resistance to modern ideas or methods, the people cling tenaciously to old traditions and beliefs.

No respect is paid to women, the birth of a daughter being considered a misfortune. The average Chinese girl has no education, but is a slave to her family until, without any regard for her own wishes, a husband is chosen, when she must devote herself to his people.

Only the higher classes of women have bandaged feet, a practice which is gradually decreasing.

The quaint little woman shown here is a member of the middle class. Her costume comprises a scant petticoat of heavy green silk, over which are two tunics with large, loose sleeves. The under tunic is of blue satin, the upper of yellow silk bordered with crimson.

At the recent tour of China's foremost statesman, Li Hung Chang, it was a noteworthy fact that he went out of his way to visit the great Singer factories, where he proved himself to be a domesticated man. Seated at one of the machines, he carefully stitched a seam, and was moved, for the first and only time during his tour, to give an order.

Such is the reputation of Singer Sewing Machines even in unprogressive China.

Sold on Instalments
You can try one FREE
Old Machines taken in Exchange

THE SINGER MANUFACTURING COMPANY
Offices in Every City in the World

Figure 3.19   Singer National Costume Series, "China," Singer advertisement from *Harper's Magazine Advertiser,* 1899. (Collection of the author)

SINGER National Costume Series

RUSSIA

RUSSIA, the most extensive empire ever established, stretches from a land in the south where the vine and fig flourish, to the barren, frozen plains of the Arctic region; it is peopled by more different races than any other nation.

The original tribes, the true Slavs, are physically the nearest to perfection of any people.

Three widely distinct classes exist: the nobles, the burghers or townsfolk, and the peasants.

Among such a diversity of races and social conditions the costumes are necessarily very different. The photograph shows a traveling salesman, clad in the loose, flowing, priestly robe largely worn by men of the middle class in Central European Russia, explaining to a customer the use of a Singer sewing machine.

The woman wears the indoor costume of the women of Novgorod, a long, loose, richly embroidered robe over which is a long, open, sleeveless jacket. Her gold beads and sequins are considered family heirlooms.

Singer sewing machines are distributed throughout the vast Russian Empire, and Singer offices are found in every town of any importance. Thus, this product of American genius is bringing the women of the whole world into one universal kinship and sisterhood.

Sold on Instalments.   You can try one FREE.
Old machines taken in Exchange.

The Singer Manufacturing Company
Offices in Every City in the World.

Figure 3.20   Singer National Costume Series, "Russia," Singer advertisement from *McClure's Magazine,* 1899. (Collection of the author)

its treatment of women. Similarly, the ad labeled "Turkey (Albania)" included a paragraph explicitly about women: "The women are mere slaves, tall and strong, uneducated, and ill-treated. The introduction of Singer sewing machines into this country has proved a great blessing to its women who make all the garments worn by the family, and deftly produce the embroidery which forms one of the chief exports." Russia, on the other hand, is presented in its "costume" ad without reference to the plight of its women; the bulk of the text pertains to the diversity of the Russian empire and its styles of clothing. Particularly interesting in this ad is the summation statement, where Singer makes explicit its claims: "Singer sewing machines are distributed throughout the vast Russian Empire, and Singer offices are found in every town of any importance. Thus, this product of American genius is bringing the women of the whole world into one universal kinship and sisterhood." In other words, American technology in the guise of the sewing machine was helping to erase differences between women, joining them through their participation in a proper domestic activity (see Figure 3.21). For some women, that "proper" feminine activity was also potentially liberating. Sewing on Singer machines liberated some women (such as those from Turkey and China) by allowing them to engage in the paid workforce and therefore lose their dependence (as "slaves") on men; others, such as American women, were

Figure 3.21 "All Nations Sing the Praises," Singer advertisement from *Century Magazine,* circa 1898. (Collection of the author)

liberated by the "labor-saving" that the machines provided, freeing them, as the "Woman's Century" ads suggested, to participate in golfing or teaching. H.J. Heinz Company also drew on this theme of liberating women from the drudgery of housework. In many of their advertisements, women are told that they will be able to perform domestic work much more efficiently if they purchase manufactured food products. In fact, the "Heinz Girl" featured in many of the company's ads is depicted as a domestic servant, donning a white cap and apron, ready to help the woman of the house complete her "duties" (see Figure 5.4).

In these various appeals to women, Singer reinforced what some would say was the contradictory position of women in turn-of-the-century America. Women's traditional roles as society's keepers of values and morality, the cult of true womanhood, was seen by many as potentially empowering because it gave women a public role through their "feminine influences." Thus, as scholars have shown, many middle-class women were able to move onto the public stage by participating in activities that were seen as extensions of their traditional domestic roles — such as working in settlement houses, in city beautification efforts, and as missionaries.[33] Women readers of Singer's ads found themselves in similar situations. As domestic seamstresses, they were participants in the cult of true womanhood, *and* they were participants in the civilizing process overseas by purchasing and using a product that was helping women to progress beyond "slavery." An 1897 ad (Figure 3.22) highlights the "universal" power of women's "influence." The image draws on a common motif of Singer advertising — portraying the world as a globe that is topped by or surrounded by a sewing machine. But here, the text adds a more direct message: "Woman's influence envelopes the world through the use of the Singer, the universal sewing machine." Again, Singer drew on and reinforced many middle-class women's understandings of their important role in shaping political and moral life.

This position of American women vis-à-vis their "sisters" overseas was similar of course to that of British women, many of whom gained considerable personal and political power through their "feminine" influences in colonization and who, in turn, used their work overseas to legitimize their political positions at home.[34] In the United States, as Louise Newman has shown, suffrage movements in the late 19th and early 20th centuries drew on a related discourse that positioned African-Americans and Native Americans as less than civilized and in need of women's civilizing influence.[35] Singer's ads could be read in a similar light. In this way, these advertisements reflected a discourse of women's rights that was right down the middle

Figure 3.22 "Woman's Influence Envelopes the World," Singer advertisement from *Century Magazine*, 1897. (Collection of the author)

of political consciousness — that women had some power, but it was a power based on their essential sexual difference from men.

Given the complexity of the political and social conversations regarding sexual difference that were circulating in late 19th and early 20th century America, it is not surprising that Singer's advertisements contained multiple messages about women's position in American society. After 1900, Singer created ads that de-essentialized women's differences from men. This was partly due, no doubt, to the changing sociocultural climate and the rise of the "new woman." But it also developed from Singer's rhetorical commitments to the idea of progress. As we have seen, integral to Singer's ethos of international sales was a notion of unfixed racial differences — of the malleability of subjectivity. Applying this ethos to sexual difference, women could be thought of as evolving and becoming less different than men. In this way, Singer could simultaneously portray its belief in progress as measured by the status of women around the world while appealing to the "new" woman at home; it could be modern and traditional at the same time.

Thus, throughout the first decade of the 20th century, as Singer was making its largest and most significant forays overseas — "civilizing" "other" women through consumption — its advertising campaigns at home focused more and more on American women's accomplishments and progress. The "Woman's Century" ads discussed earlier can be interpreted in this light, although these ads still featured images of "traditional" women. In the first decades of the 20th century, Singer removed all such references. For example, an interesting series of trade cards that were produced by Singer featured photos of, and some taken by, Annie Peck on her various mountaineering trips in South America. Annie Peck was an adventurer who dedicated the second part of her life to mountain climbing in Peru and Bolivia. She was constantly in need of financial support and sought what would today be called "corporate sponsorship." Apparently, Singer obliged. After the publicity surrounding her first major climb in 1895, Singer issued a set of cards depicting Peck posed in her climbing gear, a daring outfit that included knickers and boots — a far cry from the petticoats that were required of women on the streets.[36] As a contemporary commentator noted: "Ladies pumping away at the treadle could sigh with admiration at one of their sex who had launched into the world's more daring occupation."[37] Later, in 1908, Singer produced a series of cards that featured photos taken by Peck during her various trips. These were large cards (4½ by 7¼ inches) suitable for framing and were marked with the copyright of Annie S. Peck, who presumably was paid for their use. The back of these cards

MOUNT HUASCARAN FROM A
HEIGHT OF 10,000 FEET

OUNT HUASCARAN, as seen from the hills 2,000 feet above Yungay, is of wonderful grandeur. Of the long range of snow-clad giants this is the most dazzling and glorious. It has been measured as 22,600 feet and also as 25,000 feet above the sea.

From my own observations the snow-line would seem to be at a height of 15,000 feet, the top of the saddle 20,000 and the summit of the south peak, probably the higher, 23,000 or 24,000 feet.

If but 23,000 the mountain will still be higher than Aconcagua, hence the loftiest known summit on this hemisphere; if 24,000 feet its ascent breaks the world's record.

All of these pictures are from photographs taken by Miss Peck on her recent expedition to Peru.

Singer Talks to Men With Wives Who Sew

❡ There are certain things that men would better leave alone—the wives know more about them than you do.

❡ This is probably true of sewing machines, and yet while you may cheerfully let your wife make a small mistake, you would dislike to see her spend many dollars for a sewing machine that might be next to useless within a year.

❡ Women seek "bargains" even more than do men, and the makers and sellers of poorly constructed sewing machines use a "cheap" price to tempt trade because they dare not make a true statement of quality.

❡ Therefore, urge your wife at least TO LEARN about the Singer before she spends her money for a machine which appears to be a bargain because offered at a lower price.

❡ Singer reputation is backed by fifty years' experience; Singer sales exceed the sales of ALL others combined.

Figure 3.23 Flip side of Singer card with photo by Annie Peck of Mount Huascaran in Peru, circa 1908. (Collection of the author)

contained information about the photograph — where it was taken, what sort of geographical facts it depicted — followed at the bottom by the Singer section, which consisted of either the Singer logo, advertising its latest machine design, or textual information. One card had a list of four points under the title "Singer Talks to Thinking Women," and another "Singer Talks to Men with Wives Who Sew" (see Figure 3.23). Although these points made no explicit reference to the accomplishments of the "new" woman (such as mountaineering), the implicit association was there: "thinking" women used Singer machines.

This is not to say, of course, that the Singer Company was promoting women's rights in the United States or was working to challenge the dominant views of a fixed racial hierarchy. However, its very practical economic view of the world's potential consumers, driven by its need for increased profits and combined with the evolutionary notion of continuous change that was integral to the discourse of civilization — that is, that peoples' subjectivities could change through time — created a corporate world view of malleable identities, applicable to other races and both sexes. At the same time, however, Singer's advertisements reinforced other forms of identity that were not malleable. Foreign women could become more "modern" and "civilized" by using the Singer machine, but they were always placed clearly outside the American nation, dressed in exotic, "native" clothing. By maintaining geographical distance, Singer found it safe to portray foreign peoples of other races becoming "civilized" through consumption — they could be presented within a patriarchal family, in proper domestic surroundings, using the tools of modernity. These foreign peoples, then, could be depicted as becoming almost "white" and American.

Endnotes

1. J.S. Ingram, *The Centennial Exposition, Described and Illustrated* (Philadelphia: Hubbard Brothers, 1876), 159.
2. At the end of the Civil War, Singer's exports were approximately 40% of its total sales, and by 1879 foreign sales outnumbered domestic sales. See Robert Bruce Davies, *Peacefully Working to Conquer the World: Singer Sewing Machines in Foreign Markets, 1854–1920* (New York: Arno Press, 1976), 39; Mira Wilkins, *The Emergence of Multinational Enterprise: American Business Abroad from the Colonial Era to 1914* (Cambridge, MA: Harvard University Press, 1970), 43; Fred V. Carstensen, *American Enterprise in Foreign Markets: Studies of Singer and International Harvester in Imperial Russia* (Chapel Hill, NC: University of North Carolina Press, 1984), 24.
3. Robert W. Rydell, *All the World's a Fair: Visions of Empire at American International Expositions, 1876–1916* (Chicago: University of Chicago Press, 1984), 22.
4. James Dabney McCabe, *The Illustrated History of the Centennial Exhibition* (Philadelphia: National Publishing Company, 1876), 632.
5. Ibid., 632.
6. Charles M. Gilmore, *The Herald Guide Book and Directory to the Centennial International Exhibition* (Philadelphia: Charles Gilmore, 1876), 18.

7. Gilmore (1876), 18.
8. "The Singer Manufacturing Co. at the Exposition," *Halligan's Illustrated World's Fair*, 5 (October 1893): 672.
9. From the exhibit brochure "The Singer Manufacturing Company's Exhibit of Family Sewing Machines and Art Embroidery," 1893.
10. Ibid.
11. Ibid.
12. Ibid.
13. *Halligan's Illustrated World's Fair*, 5 (October 1893): 672.
14. *Halligan's Illustrated World's Fair*, 5 (December 1893): 732.
15. Ibid., 733.
16. Ibid., 733.
17. Ibid., 732.
18. Singer Exhibit brochure.
19. Ibid.
20. Davies (1976), 99.
21. See, for example, Jan Pieterse, *White on Black: Images of Africa and Blacks in Western Popular Culture* (New Haven, CT: Yale University Press, 1990); Jackson Lears, *Fables of Abundance: A Cultural History of Advertising in America* (New York: Basic Books, 1995); M. Mehaffy, "Advertising Race: Raceing Advertising: The Feminine Consumer (-Nation), 1876–1900," *Signs*, 23 (1997): 131–174.
22. Anne McClintock, *Imperial Leather: Race, Gender, and Sexuality in the Colonial Contest* (New York: Routledge, 1995), 223.
23. Ibid., 222.
24. Ibid., 225.
25. Ibid., 222.
26. Ibid., 222.
27. Ibid., 223.
28. The "war" reference apparently alludes to the reputation of the Zulu people as good warriors, a stereotype that had been popularized in the United States.
29. Susan Schulten, *The Geographical Imagination in America, 1880–1950* (Chicago: University of Chicago Press, 2001).
30. Henry Adams, *The Education of Henry Adams: An Autobiography* (Norwalk, CT: The Heritage Press, 1970), 319.
31. Rydell (1984), 63.
32. Quoted in ibid., 252.
33. See, for example, Ann Douglas, *The Feminization of American Culture* (New York: Doubleday, 1988); Dolores Hayden, *The Grand Domestic Revolution: A History of Feminist Designs for American Homes, Neighborhoods, and Cities* (Cambridge, MA: MIT Press, 1981); M. Christine Boyer, *Dreaming the Rational City: The Myth of American City Planning* (Cambridge, MA: The MIT Press, 1990).
34. See Vron Ware, *Beyond the Pale: White Women, Racism, and History* (New York: Verso Books, 1992); Antoinette M. Burton, *Burdens of History: British Feminists, Indian Women, and Imperial*

Culture, 1865–1915 (Chapel Hill, NC: University of North Carolina Press, 1994).

35. Louise Michele Newman, *White Women's Rights: The Racial Origins of Feminism in the United States* (New York: Oxford University Press, 1999).

36. For the full and fascinating story of Annie Smith Peck, see Elizabeth Faggs Olds, *Women of the Four Winds: The Adventures of Four of America's First Women Explorers* (Boston: Houghton Mifflin, 1985).

37. Quoted in ibid., 12.

4

Manliness and McCormick: Frontier Narratives in Foreign Lands

Along with the familiar themes of conquering a "wilderness" and making homes upon the land, Turner emphasized another, less familiar, theme: in advancing the frontier, a diverse people of European origins had remade themselves into Americans. Turner had extended the meaning of progress. Progress was not merely an increase in material well-being but was cultural as well: growing democracy, greater equality, more opportunity.
—Richard White, "Frederick Jackson Turner and Buffalo Bill," in *The Frontier in American Culture,* ed. James R. Grossman (Berkeley: University of California Press, 1994), 12–13.

In the grand march of human progress which distinguishes the present age above all others, agricultural machinery occupies a prominent position, being second to none in its important bearing on the well-being of society. It has released the farmer from the drudgery of life, almost miraculously increased the production of food, and so far reduced its cost that the human family to-day is better fed and better clothed than at any time in all its previous history. In Australia, New Zealand, North and South Africa, in Russia, Italy, France, Spain, Greece and Great Britain, as well as in the republics of South America, the McCormick machines is as well known, highly appreciated and eagerly sought after as on the prairies of Illinois.... The McCormick is at home in a foreign harvest field, and needs no introduction or interpreter, for its work speaks in all languages throughout the circuit of the earth.
— McCormick catalog, 1885

McCormick Harvesting Machine Company's advertising strategies in the late 19th century drew on a powerful set of images and story lines about American character and the American frontier that we now associate with Turner's famous 1893 essay "The Significance of the Frontier in American History." As Richard White has argued, one of Turner's key ideas was that the process of settling the frontier actively shaped character.[1] In other words, American-ness could be attained from recapitulating the march of pioneers into the uninhabited wilderness, bringing progress and civilization in the form of agriculture and proper domesticity. The frontier narrative, then, gave a particularly American "spin" to the discourse of civilization because it specified exactly how American culture had reached the top of the civilizational hierarchy (through the domestication of wilderness). White also argued that this set of ideas was "already conventional" and familiar to most Americans by the time Turner's address was delivered. "The iconography of the frontier," White argues, "had already prepared his audience to accept these bold claims as mere common sense."[2]

This "iconography of the frontier," as the second quote above makes clear, was also used to sell farm equipment. McCormick aligned its products with the "grand march of progress" across the United States, helping to create the American character. As Figure 4.1, an 1886 advertising poster shows, McCormick literally inserted itself into America's storyline of westward expansion. The company also extended the metaphor beyond the borders of the United States, as it presented images and words in its catalogs and other advertising material that showed how the Americanization process of the frontier was being recapitulated in "foreign harvest fields ... throughout the circuit of the earth." McCormick machines, whose work "speaks in all languages," were remaking all farmers who used them into Americans, whether in "Russia, Italy, France, Spain, Greece." According to this advertising text, the translation from the American West to frontiers overseas was complete, with "no introduction or interpreter" needed. In fact, even though the work of McCormick's machinery may have spoken "in all languages" with no need for an interpreter, the company's catalogs definitely did need translation. McCormick began to print its catalogs in different languages as early as 1870 in order to accommodate the German, Swedish, and Norwegian speakers of the upper Midwest and Great Plains regions. By the 1890s, with overseas sales increasing, the company printed their catalogs in more than 10 languages.

McCormick certainly was not unique in using the iconography of the frontier to promote its products, but it was the first to translate this set of ideas beyond American borders. By doing so, it both reiterated

Figure 4.1   "Westward the Course of Empire Takes Its Way with McCormick in the Van," McCormick Advertising Poster, circa 1886. (Wisconsin Historical Society, WHi-2496)

the set of meanings contained within and created new meanings. By shifting the frontier story into lands beyond the United States, and beyond American territorial and political interests, the story itself was transformed. The "emigrants" of the American story became the inhabitants of other countries, and the process of progress shifted from a primarily spatial story (the occupation and settlement of the wilderness) to a temporal one (the consumption and use of modern machinery). In other words, the mechanism that created the "American character" in the first instance was the actual work of transforming wilderness; the mechanism of change in the second instance was the use of modern machinery.

This chapter traces the various ways that McCormick Harvesting Machine Company, and its successor, International Harvester (IH), incorporated and legitimized its international sales by drawing on and reshaping the discourse of civilization and the frontier narrative in its advertising materials. Farm equipment as a commodity lent itself to the civilizational discourse. Like the sewing machine, harvesters were new types of machinery, signs of modernity that considerably lessened the amount of manual labor involved in agriculture. And like sewing machines, farm machines were being exported from the United States to Europe, Central and South America, and parts of Asia from the late 19th century on. Despite the obvious differences in these two products — the marketing of farm machines of course was geared toward men, sewing machines toward women — the stories their advertising told about the rest of the world were amazingly similar: other peoples of the world were becoming "civilized" through their use of American products. But these stories took on a particular hue given the particular meanings and uses of farm equipment. Unlike Singer's advertising, which contained stories of otherness that focused on individual cultural traits, such as clothing, and whose discourse of civilization focused on the details of domesticity, McCormick's advertising focused on stages of economic development at the scale of the nation, and its language drew as much on notions of progress as on civilization. The Jeffersonian symbol of American identity — the yeoman in the garden — was well suited to play a starring role in farm machinery advertising. An American man sitting atop a McCormick harvester served to associate McCormick with the highest ideals of civilization — manly men working with modern machinery, producing food and wealth to support their wives and children. It also proved to be extremely adaptable imagery, as the "frontier" of McCormick shifted from the American West to areas beyond. Farm equipment was presented as the means for turning the wilderness abroad into civilization and shaping foreigners into Americans, or at least American consumer-subjects.

The Grand McCormick March of Human Progress

McCormick's first catalog, printed in 1859, contained mostly figure drawings that were accompanied by descriptive text about each of the company's products. Its back cover, however, was a black-and-white print that told its own story (see Figure 4.2). The image shows two men in, presumably, a wheat field who are operating a threshing machine; a third man on horseback points toward a characteristic midcentury Midwestern farmhouse — a greek-revival–styled upright and wing house, beautifully decorated with ornate cornices and a front porch. The surrounding landscape includes rolling hills with hedgerows between agricultural fields, a lake with sailboats, and a small river or stream running in front of the house. The house itself sits amidst a grove of deciduous trees. Although Greenville, Minnesota, is printed underneath the artist's name, it is difficult to say for certain whether that refers to the home of the artist, or the place depicted in the image itself. What is important here is the connection between the men working in their fields using farm machinery and the beautiful house in the distance, an image that makes visual and concrete the Jeffersonian ideal for America — the yeoman in his garden, with his white house surrounded by a grove of trees.[3]

Figure 4.2 Back cover, McCormick's 1859 catalog. (Wisconsin Historical Society, WHi-36140)

This quintessential image of American identity foreshadows what was to be found in one form or another in all McCormick catalogs, although, as we will see, the location of this "yeoman in the garden" changed over time.

In the late 1870s and particularly the 1880s, McCormick Company's yearly catalogs began to showcase the company's overseas sales, using its "world dominance" to advertise its products, even though, as discussed in chapter 2, its export market really did not reach its peak until the first decade of the 20th century. The company also began to publish its catalogs using chromolithographs on its front and back cover, making them visually striking (in color) and collectible. Other farm machinery companies also created visually interesting catalogs and boasted of their international prominence, particularly Deering Harvester Company and Buckeye Mower and Reaper Company, but fitting with its increasing dominance over the national and international markets, McCormick's catalogs maintained a consistently high quality of design. Its 1878 catalog, with a cover image similar to its 1859 catalog, focused on "its record in New Zealand" and reported on its recent success at the 1878 Paris Exposition (see Figure 4.3). Together, these two "events" provided occasion for the company to boast of its new international status: "To give some idea of the popularity of our machines in that distant land, and of the magnitude of the trade we have just opened up there, [we] would say that these machines, loaded at our works, filled one hundred and sixteen freight cars — *the largest shipment of agricultural implements,*

Figure 4.3   Front cover, McCormick's 1878 catalog. (Wisconsin Historical Society, WHi-36142)

we venture to say, *ever made at one time on a single order* from any establishment in the world" (emphasis in original). With sales in several European countries, and this new market in New Zealand, the company felt emboldened to say that it had circled the globe and brought with it progress and civilization: "After almost half a century of close and uninterrupted attention to this, our sole business, it is gratifying to be able to announce that we have at last circled the globe with the triumphs of the McCormick machines; that we have been permitted to add something to the world's industry and progress, and in some measure to have alleviated the toils of the husbandmen at home and abroad." This notion of encircling the globe soon took on symbolic status. In the company's 1880 catalog, the words "world renowned" became part of the company logo, and in 1881, a globe was added, with the phrase "McCormick's World Renowned Machinery" stretched across it. This global symbol of the company recurred often in the next 20 years.

Filling out this "global" vision were spatial and temporal narratives of progress. The 1883 catalog introduced two of these stories. The first was a spatial story of progress. In a section titled "Magnitude of the McCormick Business," the extent of McCormick's business is aligned with the spatial expansion of the United States, a sort of manifest destiny of machinery:

> The great increase in the manufacture of McCormick machines within the past thirty years, and especially within the last ten years, is on a par with the astonishingly rapid spread of population over the vast regions under the glorious flag of the United States, and but for the invention of the reaping machine, the gigantic and extended scale of farming of the present day would be a sheer impossibility. In less than thirty-five years the plow and the reaper have enabled the tide of emigration to push its way across the continent, and establish an empire between the Mississippi and the Oregon, where, but for these agencies, the red man would still hold undisputed sway.

As this quote makes clear, McCormick aligned its own success in selling machines with the westward migration of farmers "under the glorious flag of the United States," making farming possible in land where the "red man" had held "sway." As the next several sentences suggest, this new empire of McCormick was becoming even more expansive:

> In 1849 there were but 1,500 McCormick machines built, and their sale did not extend beyond the then newly organized States of Iowa and Wisconsin; the territory westward being literally a wilderness. In 1882 our sales numbered over

48,000 machines, sold wherever grain and grass are grown, throughout the civilized world. The farmer in Great Britain, France, Russia, Northern and Southern Africa, South America, New Zealand and Australia is as familiar with the click of the McCormick Reaper as the farmer of Illinois.

Here, the areas outside the United States are seen simply as extensions of the American westward movement and are culturally no different —areas that use the McCormick are considered part of the "civilized world."

This spatial story of progress was bolstered with a temporal story. Near the end of the catalog was a two-page visual spread titled "The Evolution of the Reaper and Survival of the Fittest" (see Figure 4.4). In this piece, Darwinian notions of evolution are twinned with civilizational discourse in order to equate the evolution of the reaper with the evolution of society, from primitive to civilized. Modern farm machinery liberates women from manual labor (see the second stage) and creates modern, efficient forms of farming — all signs of "civilization." A comparison of the "first stage" and the "sixth stage" is particularly telling. The first stage shows a farm in disrepair, with pigs — seemingly in charge here — that have toppled over fences and a farmer who has only his own manual labor to protect and harvest his grains. In the sixth stage, 1883, the world of "today," everything is in its place. There is no doubt who is in charge — the farmer sits tall atop the latest McCormick binder, able to survey his fields. The pigs are in their place, outside the frame of the center image, dead and hanging to dry in orderly fashion, while the reaping hook, rake, and scythe have been in disuse so long that spider webs have formed between their handles. This set of images also shows the application of evolutionary ideas to legitimize the business success of McCormick — the company has succeeded because it is the "fittest;" the machine has triumphed through a series of struggles and therefore is "naturally" the best.

Taken together, these two stories of progress project an image of McCormick as triumphant over time and space. The machines are both the endpoint of evolution (the fittest) and have helped bring about that evolution. They conquered wilderness and brought American-style civilization to the West and beyond. These two parallel stories remain the dominant motifs for McCormick advertising throughout the late 19th and early 20th centuries.

The 1884 catalog provides further elaboration. The cover image (see Figure 4.5) builds on the 1883 "evolution" schema, as it contrasts an image of the past, the focus of the picture, with an image of the present — the yeoman farmer atop his harvesting machine (shown at

Figure 4.4 "The Evolution of the Reaper and the Survival of the Fittest," McCormick's 1883 catalog, 22–23. (Wisconsin Historical Society, WHi-36161 and 36163)

Figure 4.4 (continued)

the bottom of the picture). Without even reading the accompanying text, the reader easily knows that this center image depicts the past — the spider webs on the scythe are again used as important clues, but the figures in the middle also indicate a less-than-modern scenario.

Figure 4.5 Front cover, McCormick's 1884 catalog. (Wisconsin Historical Society, WHi-4396)

Manual labor instead of machines, oxen instead of horses, and the figure dressed in unusual clothes, particularly his headgear, all indicate a contrast with the present. The text makes certain the time and place: "Reaper used by Ancient Gauls, First Century."

This depiction of the past, showing by contrast the superiority of the McCormick machine, sets the tone of the story told within this catalog. Its first section, titled "A Retrospect," opens with a sentence that reiterates the Jeffersonian ideal: "Agriculture is the noblest employment of man, and is the true source of a nation's prosperity and independence." This is followed by a narrative of the settlement of the United States similar to the 1883 catalog; however, this time, the narrative moves into a consideration of the links between agricultural success and other economic ventures:

> Consider for a moment that less than twenty-five years ago, the United States were compelled to import wheat to support our people! While now, the farmers of this goodly land produce over five hundred million bushels of wheat, and can easily export two hundred millions of it in exchange for foreign gold or the products of foreign soil, thus enriching our people and stimulating them to still greater efforts. In view of these facts, who can estimate the progress of this country in the next quarter century?

This narrative suggests that McCormick machines, by exponentially increasing wheat harvests, have led to American prosperity and will continue to do so in the future. On page 5, the narrative turns to a depiction of McCormick's spatial expansion:

> The success of the McCormick machine is a wonder, and still the wonder grows. The boom rolls on, and like a mighty avalanche it grows as it rolls, until 50,000 machines a year does not now suffice to satisfy demand, a demand that comes up from every portion of the earth where the summer sun ripens the golden grain, until we recognize our harvest field to be the world, while our patrons and friends are to be found in every clime. Indeed so world-wide is the use of this machine in both Northern and Southern Hemispheres, that is can be truthfully said, the Sun never sets on the work of the McCormick Reaper throughout the entire year.

And on page 7, McCormick forecasts more progress in the form of better machines:

> We are well aware that the intelligent farmers all concede that today we produce harvesting machines that are far ahead of our rivals in all the elements and combinations of a first class

machine. Yet we never rest, but year by year the work of improving goes on and our motto is still "Onward."

All three of these quotes suggest the degree to which movement, advancement, and progress — an evolutionary view of time and space — infiltrated the discourse of McCormick.

The 1885 catalog echoes these themes. It opens with the quote at the beginning of this chapter: "In the grand march of human progress which distinguishes the present age above all others, agricultural machinery occupies a prominent position, being second to none in its important bearing on the well-being of society." This "grand march" onward is used to describe change at a variety of scales — the improvement of human society, but also the improvement of machinery. McCormick explicitly invokes evolutionary language to portray its own course of improvement:

Those who have watched the history of reaper building know that the pathway of improvement is strewn with the wrecks of machines whose names live now only in the records of the Patent Office.... The inexorable law of the survival of the fittest has retired many a machine from the market in years gone by and is bound to retire many more in the near future.

The "inexorable law of the survival of the fittest" is here used to prompt farmers to buy only the latest McCormick machines, which are clearly superior to those "whose names live ... only in the records" because they represent the best that civilization can offer. These new 1885 machines were not necessarily the endpoint of this "pathway of improvement," however; as McCormick made sure to suggest, newer and better machines were to follow. In this way, the company used evolutionary language to legitimize what we today would call "planned obsolescence" — the old must inevitably make way for the new.

Having aligned its latest machines with the evolutionary pathway of improvement, therefore indicating their superiority to anything that came before, the catalog ended by returning to its opening discussion of McCormick machines as the "avant couriers of civilization." The last section was titled "Its world-wide fame" and included a discussion of all the areas in the world where McCormick machines were "well known, highly appreciated and eagerly sought after." A farmer reading the catalog, then, could assume that purchasing a McCormick machine associated him with the highest level of civilization — not

Figure 4.6 "Treading Out the Grain in Oriental Style," McCormick's 1885 catalog. (Wisconsin Historical Society, WHi-36198)

only were the machines themselves the best that evolutionary processes could offer, they were also bringing civilization to others in the world, fulfilling the millennial vision of moving toward perfect, civilized societies. This catalog section ends by stressing how easily McCormick machines move through the world: "The McCormick is at home in a foreign harvest field, and needs no introduction or interpreter, for its work speaks in all languages throughout the circuit of the earth." An interesting image that appears at the end of the catalog, titled "Treading out the grain in oriental style," shows that McCormick's "work" is not yet spoken everywhere (see Figure 4.6). In this image, grain is being treaded, or stamped down, not by machinery, but by the rather chaotic movements of horses, with the rest of the work to be done by manual laborers, including women (background, center left), a sure sign of a culture not yet civilized. Similar to the narrative that McCormick created about the trajectory of improvement of its machines, a trajectory that was to continue into the future, this image suggested the future of the "march of human progress" into the "Oriental" world.

It is not clear what exactly McCormick Company meant by the term "Oriental," but if the 1886 catalog is any indication, the reference was to India. Much of the text of this catalog was dedicated to telling the historical narrative of wheat and wheat reaping, or what McCormick titled "A short history of wheat and wheat reapers in ancient and modern times." The purpose of telling this story, as is made clear early on, is to contrast the difficulties of reaping wheat in the past with the great improvements made by McCormick machines. As the narrative develops, however, it becomes apparent that the contrast is also between the "Orient" and the "Occident." In this use of what Anne McClintock would call "anachronistic space," a past stage of "society" is projected into a "foreign" place.[4] In this case, that place is India. McCormick's focus on India is not difficult to understand. The inside back cover of the catalog directs the reader to a colored chart that shows very clearly (see Figure 4.7) the amount of wheat harvested in different countries. After the United States and France, the next highest producer of wheat is India. Clearly, then, India presented a large and untapped market for the McCormick Harvesting Machine Company. Depictions of the primitive methods of harvesting wheat there became a common motif for the company, one it used throughout the decade as an advertising tool.

McCormick's history of wheat harvesting is a history of technology, presented in stages. The historical narrative starts with a discussion of how different peoples around the world traditionally harvested wheat throughout time; for the most part, the technologies they used were basic and primitive. In the first stage, during the Stone, Bronze, and Iron Ages, "long before the Christian era," people developed and used different forms of sickles and primitive scythes. At this point in the narrative, the discussion of the past — of time — is automatically transformed into a discussion of space. By so doing, foreign space is aligned with the premodern, with Western's civilization's past. In Anne McClintock's words, "The axis of time was projected onto the axis of space and history became global."[5] At first, the catalog makes a brief mention that these types of historical tools "have been lately seen in central Hungary and in Syria." But then the story continues with a detailed vignette, complete with image, of reaping wheat in India: "At the present day the farmer in India has no better reaper than a piece of hard iron, six inches in length, curved like an old-fashioned sickle, with a notched edge and a short handle, the cost of the tool being four cents. He sits upon his heels, cuts a handful of straw, which he lays carefully down, and then waddles on without rising, cutting in this way about one-twelfth an acre a day." The image shows a man with a head wrap dressed only from the waist down, stooping while using his sickle to harvest a small sheath of wheat (see Figure 4.8).

After this "aside," the historical story continues, moving on to the first century Gauls, who apparently had developed a more advanced

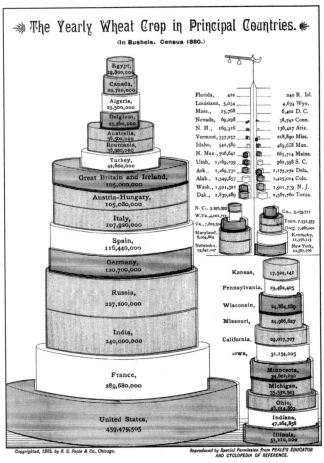

Figure 4.7 "The Yearly Wheat Crop in Principal Countries," McCormick's 1886 catalog. (Wisconsin Historical Society, WHi-36206)

technology — a wagon with a type of sickle attached to it so that when it was pushed by an ox into stalks of wheat, the wheat would be cut and fall into the wagon. This story too was accompanied by a figure drawing that showed this wagon in use, with a man — looking extremely similar to the one reaping in India (head wrap, shirtless) — helping to cut the wheat (see Figure 4.8). The figure in ancient Gaul is here equated with a present day Indian — both are depicted using primitive technologies to harvest wheat. From the ancient Gauls, the story moves quickly, in less than a paragraph, to the first mechanical reaper in Great Britain, and then, of course, to Cyrus McCormick, the founder of McCormick Harvesting Machine Company.

Figure 4.8 "Reaping Wheat in India" (top) and "Reaper of the Ancient Gauls in First Century," (bottom), McCormick's 1886 catalog, 5. (Wisconsin Historical Society, WHi-36203)

This same story, told without words, is replicated in a small brochure from the same year (see Figure 4.9). The first page (top, right) is comprised of three images — reaper of the ancient Gauls in first century (identical to the catalog image), the gleaners (women picking up wheat in the fields), and a small image of a sickle from the iron age. The three lithographs on the second page (bottom, left) depict other, more recent, reaping technologies: a man using a reaping hook, a grain cradle and, at the bottom, two men operating McCormick's first reaper of 1831. Page 4 (top, left) offers two large images of the most recent McCormick products in use but centers on a smaller image, identical to the one in the catalog, called "Reaping wheat in India, the only method pursued at the present time." The implication of this final page is clear: Indian farmers were currently using primitive farming methods, but the course of history and evolution would lead these primitive methods to give way to modern ones. In sum, this brochure put into pictures the entire McCormick narrative of progress.

The 1887 catalog carried on this theme of historical progress, with a specific emphasis on progress measured by the reordering of nature. This theme (progress being measured not only by a stage

Figure 4.9   "Reaper of the Ancient Gauls in First Century," McCormick advertising brochure, 1886. (Wisconsin Historical Society, WHi-36208 and 36369)

Figure 4.10 "The McCormick in Asiatic Russia," McCormick's 1887 catalog, 29. (Wisconsin Historical Society, WHi-36371)

of human activity and gender specialization, but by the degree of manipulation of nature) is common to the discourse of civilization as far back as the Enlightenment. The word "civilization" itself is historically related to cultivation — to the "taming" of the earth under the supervision of human hands.[6] And, certainly, the marketing of farm equipment lent itself to this theme. The opening paragraph of McCormick's 1887 catalog measures the success of the reaping machine by the degree to which it, along with other modern inventions, is responsible for altering the earth:

> But the last half century has seen a great awakening the world over. Within that period more important inventions have been put in operation than in all the ages preceding; inventions that have not only changed the mode of living, but changed to a great extent the surface of the earth, and surrounded mankind with entirely different influences and environments. Railroads, steamboats, telegraphs, reaping machines and a host of minor inventions have, by their combined influence, set the world in a blaze of excitement and upon a career of marvelous prosperity and improvement.

This altering of "the surface of the earth" and the resulting creation of different "environments" led in turn to more "prosperity and improvement." This quote, therefore, reiterates a common theme in Victorian attitudes toward nature: cultivating the earth through mechanical means was a both a sign of civilization and a means of attaining it. The two images that accompany this narrative depict the

Figure 4.11 "The McCormick in Italy," McCormick's 1887 catalog, 31. (Wisconsin Historical Society, WHi-36373)

spread of this mechanical manipulation of nature "the world over." The first image portrays McCormick machines being used in Asiatic Russia (see Figure 4.10); the second, in Italy (see Figure 4.11). Both images resemble in form the figure of harvesting in Dakota that appeared in McCormick's 1884 catalog — a flat and relatively open landscape being worked by a consecutive line of reaping machines, all producing neat bundles of grain placed at exact intervals (see Figure 4.12). These images clearly show the changes in the "surface of the earth" brought about by the reaping machine, a surface that was now orderly and almost geometric; almost, then, like the grid pattern of the American West, created by its township and range survey system. Here, Italy and Russia — two countries not considered at the highest rung of the civilizational ladder — are presented as almost fully modern.

Of course, these foreign farmers are not completely civilized or Americanized. Even though they are using modern machinery and saving women from hard labor, they have not fulfilled the American pastoral ideal. First and foremost, these men appear to be laborers, not yeoman farmers — that is, they do not own this land but are working for someone else, presumably, in the image of Russia, the man sitting on horseback surveilling them. The caption makes this more clear: "From a photograph taken on the estate of Ivan Pleshanow, 120 miles east of Samara, Russia, who operates five McCormick Harvesters and Binders, all drawn by camels." So too the caption for

Figure 4.12 "Harvest Scene in Dakota," McCormick's 1884 catalog. (Wisconsin Historical Society, WHi-36376)

the Italy image makes clear that these are not yeoman operating their own machines: "Exhibition of Mechanical Harvesting and Binding on the estates of Mr. Wm. Ponticelli, made by six 'Steel' Harvesters, at Cordicella." The work animals also point to differences. For example, the oxen depicted in Italy are reminiscent of the oxen McCormick used to represent ancient methods of cultivation, whereas the camels shown in Russia lend an exotic — "Asiatic" — flavor to these not yet American farmers.

American farmers reading through these catalogs could feel akin to these foreign farmers — after all, they were both engaged in the reordering of nature and the cultivation of the earth through mechanical means — yet slightly superior to them. Certainly, the McCormick Harvesting Machine Company created narratives in its catalogs that slipped between these two positions, sometimes reinforcing difference, other times erasing it. The cover of the 1888 catalog shows how slippery these positions were (see Figure 4.13). This picture is almost a replica of the Asiatic Russia image, but now transposed back into the United States, with workhorses instead of camels and a woman out for a leisurely ride watching from her horse. The form of the image, then, is almost identical; only the details have changed, as if the specific place and culture hardly mattered. The message, it seems, is that McCormick machines can do their work just about anywhere, ordering nature and, along with it, providing for the "march of human progress."

Figure 4.13   Front cover, McCormick's 1888 catalog. (Wisconsin Historical Society, WHi-36499)

Frontier Narratives in Foreign Lands

Near the end of the 1888 catalog McCormick provides the first specific mention of all the places where its machines are in use through the intriguing form of a monthly calendar (see Figure 4.14). Under each month is a list of the regions of the world where McCormick

JANUARY.

S	M	T	W	T	F	S
1	2	3	4	5	6	7
8	9	10	11	12	13	14
15	16	17	18	19	20	21
22	23	24	25	26	27	28
29	30	31				

The McCormick is moving ahead in Australia and New Zealand.

FEBRUARY.

S	M	T	W	T	F	S
				1	2	3	4
5	6	7	8	9	10	11
12	13	14	15	16	17	18
19	20	21	22	23	24	25
26	27	28	29			

The McCormick is working in New Zealand.

MARCH.

S	M	T	W	T	F	S
				1	2	3
4	5	6	7	8	9	10
11	12	13	14	15	16	17
18	19	20	21	22	23	24
25	26	27	28	29	30	31

The McCormick is reaping the harvest in the valleys of Mexico.

APRIL.

S	M	T	W	T	F	S
1	2	3	4	5	6	7
8	9	10	11	12	13	14
15	16	17	18	19	20	21
22	23	24	25	26	27	28
29	30					

The McCormick is occupied in Mexico, Texas and California.

MAY.

S	M	T	W	T	F	S
		1	2	3	4	5
6	7	8	9	10	11	12
13	14	15	16	17	18	19
20	21	22	23	24	25	26
27	28	29	30	31		

The McCormick is at work in Texas, Cal, Ga., Miss., the Carolinas, Ala. and Arizona.

JUNE.

S	M	T	W	T	F	S
					1	2
3	4	5	6	7	8	9
10	11	12	13	14	15	16
17	18	19	20	21	22	23
24	25	26	27	28	29	30

The McCormick is active in Kas., Mo., Va., Tenn., Ky., Ga.,Italy and Spain.

JULY.

S	M	T	W	T	F	S
1	2	3	4	5	6	7
8	9	10	11	12	13	14
15	16	17	18	19	20	21
22	23	24	25	26	27	28
29	30	31				

The McCormick is busy in Ill., Iowa, Mo., M'd. Ind., Neb.,Col., Utah.Wis., N.Y., Ohio, Mich., France, Austria, Russia and Asia.

AUGUST.

S	M	T	W	T	F	S
			1	2	3	4
5	6	7	8	9	10	11
12	13	14	15	16	17	18
19	20	21	22	23	24	25
26	27	28	29	30	31	

The McCormick is at work in Minn., Dak , Ore., Wash. Ter., Idaho France, England. Russia and Asia.

It is always Harvest Time with the McCORMICK ! While the American Farmer reads his Favorite Paper by his Winter's Fire the McCORMICK is clicking away in the Summer Sun of the Antipodes.

DECEMBER.

S	M	T	W	T	F	S
						1
2	3	4	5	6	7	8
9	10	11	12	13	14	15
16	17	18	19	20	21	22
23	24	25	26	27	28	29
30	31					

The McCormick is in the field in Australia The Argentine Republic, New Zealand and South Africa.

NOVEMBER.

S	M	T	W	T	F	S
				1	2	3
4	5	6	7	8	9	10
11	12	13	14	15	16	17
18	19	20	21	22	23	24
25	26	27	28	29	30	

The McCormick is now seen working in Southern Africa, Argentine Republic, Uruguay and Australia.

OCTOBER.

S	M	T	W	T	F	S
	1	2	3	4	5	6
7	8	9	10	11	12	13
14	15	16	17	18	19	20
21	22	23	24	25	26	27
28	29	30	31			

The McCormick is humming away in the northern portions of Dakota, Montana and Manitoba.

SEPTEMBER.

S	M	T	W	T	F	S
						1
2	3	4	5	6	7	8
9	10	11	12	13	14	15
16	17	18	19	20	21	22
23	24	25	26	27	28	29
30						

The McCormick is pushing ahead in Dakota, Montana Manitoba and Scotland.

DONOHUE & HENNEBERRY, Printers and Binders, Chicago, Ill.

Figure 4.14 "It's Always Harvest Time with the McCormick!" McCormick's 1888 catalog. (Wisconsin Historical Society, WHi-36501)

machines were used. In January, for example, "The McCormick is moving ahead in Australia and New Zealand," whereas in July, "The McCormick is busy in Illinois, Iowa, Missouri, Maryland, Indiana, Nebraska, Colorado, Utah, Wisconsin, New York, Ohio, Michigan, France, Austria, Russia and Asia." "Foreign fields" then are simply added on to the list of states as extensions of the world of the McCormick, extensions that are quantitatively but not qualitatively different than the United States. In this image, space is transposed into time; not only are McCormick reaping machines in use throughout most of the world, they are also at use throughout the calendar year, working somewhere at all times to cultivate the earth and move forward with human progress. The main caption says it all: "It is always Harvest Time with the McCormick! While the American Farmer reads his Favorite Paper by his Winter's Fire the McCormick is clicking away in the Summer Sun of the Antipodes." And *The Farmers Advance*, the name of this "favorite" paper, certainly describes what is going on: civilization in the form of mechanical harvesting methods of the McCormick is advancing through the world at all times. Those not able or willing to participate in this advancement are relegated to the sidelines of civilization, vestiges of the past, as we can see from the small inset image depicting January in New Zealand. In this vignette, a clearly "savage" man (this is connoted by his lack of proper clothing and his spear) looks on from the wilderness as civilization is being made by the McCormick. The "advance" of civilization is surely just about to take over New Zealand, so that the savage will either have to become an agriculturist, or else is doomed.

The form of this small vignette is repeated at a much grander scale on the cover of the 1889 catalog (see Figure 4.15). Here, a full-color image shows a savage warrior on horseback looking down and back toward the "march" of McCormick reapers that are "seeking new fields to conquer." The image is similar in form to many mid and late 19th century depictions of the American frontier and the march of immigrants into vast and seemingly unpopulated spaces of the West. According to Richard White, "The figure standing at the gap, or on the height or border, and watching progress unfold was one of the central American icons of the frontier. Its elements were at once relatively constant and quite flexible."[7] That flexibility is evident in this image, where the frontier is not even located in the United States, but somewhere else all together. A close reading of this image reveals the location of this new frontier. Other "savage" bodies who are participating in the "march" appear in this image — men dressed only from the waist down, with head wraps, who are tending to the oxen that are pulling the machines. From viewing past catalogs, farmers should

Figure 4.15 "Seeking New Fields to Conquer," front cover, McCormick's 1889 catalog. (Collection of the author)

have been able to identify these men as the farmers of India, about to adopt modern harvesting methods. McCormick's "new field" then seems to be India, whose primitive farmers will soon by "conquered" by the McCormick. But the warrior that dominates this image is not about to be conquered — he is presented in full regalia, on horseback,

Figure 4.16   "The Last of His Race," back cover, McCormick's 1889 catalog. (Wisconsin Historical Society, WHi-4398)

with a rifle. A warrior, not a farmer, this Indian man is presented as a vestige of the past, heading in the opposite direction from the march of "progress."

The meaning of this image is made clearer by comparing it to the image on the back cover (see Figure 4.16). Formally, both images are quite similar, with a figure dominating the foreground who represents the past, looking on at activity representing the present and future. Yet the content is quite different. From the frontier, we switch to a garden, and from India, we move to Dakota, with the now familiar five harvesters reaping in a line and a small house off in the distance. If the front image depicts the movement of the frontier, the back cover represents the next stage of civilization, the yeoman in the garden. Both the text and the image clarify the close links between these two stages. In the foreground, next to the buffalo, is a broken wagon wheel, representing the past route of immigrants who settled this area, turning this rugged nature into a civilized garden or, as the text reads, "What was only a few years ago the grazing ground of the buffalo is now the home of the McCormick." The buffalo, like the warrior on the front, and the unspoken Native American, is "the last of his race," a noble savage doomed to extinction. Taken together, these two images tell a fairly continuous story: just as American farmers, with the help of McCormick machines, turned wilderness into civilization, so too the farmers of India are turning their wilderness into civilization with the import of McCormick reapers. This, then, is a frontier narrative in a foreign land.

The differences between this foreign frontier story and the American one are telling. As scholars remind us, the American frontier story presented the wilderness as uninhabited and vacant, in need of settlement by American farmers. If Native Americans were present in these stories, they were on the sidelines looking on and were commonly considered part of nature, not humanity.[8] But in the frontier story told in the cover image here — the frontier in foreign lands — Indian farmers are depicted escorting McCormick machines into the wilderness. In other words, they are presented as active agents in the civilizing process, though clearly agents lower in the civilizational hierarchy than their Anglo "brothers" riding horseback. It is the warrior here who is positioned as the Native American, a proud but tragic figure, but one not considered a potential participant in modernity.

Packaged between this visual narrative are many pages of text describing in great detail the many parts and new devices of McCormick machines, with no verbal mention of foreign frontiers. However, each page contains a visual vignette of McCormick machines in transit, most of them in foreign lands. A farmer thumbing his way through the catalog received a visual reminder of the movement of McCormick throughout the world — a quick tour of the world, as it were — as seen by the McCormick Company. Juxtaposed with images and descriptions of the steel ledger plate, for example, is an image of McCormick machines being transported by wagon "on the road of Cortez" (see Figure 4.17), while a delivery of machines in South Africa is presented alongside drawings of tilting levers and lead wheels (see Figure 4.18). On another page, McCormick machines are shown arriving by train in Dakota. These images demonstrated that McCormick's "march of progress" across America was now being duplicated around the world, bringing civilization to foreign fields through the distribution of its machines.

The 1890 catalog makes a similar case, linking the "progress" of farmers in the United States with those around the world. The opening page depicts a clearly well-off farm couple surveying their fields, which are being harvested by a McCormick machine in the distance, almost without manual labor (see Figure 4.19). The formal aspects of this image are very similar to those that characterized a particular genre within English Georgian landscape and portraiture painting — the owners of the estate are portrayed overseeing their land, with the labor that goes into its making almost invisible.[9] This artistic "formula" became a common portraiture motif and was

Figure 4.17   "On the Road of Cortez," McCormick's 1889 catalog. (Wisconsin Historical Society, WHi-36503)

Figure 4.18   "South Africa," McCormick's 1889 catalog. (Wisconsin Historical Society, WHi-36505)

used and reiterated throughout the Anglo world for the next hundred years. In other words, this type of image was familiar to many late 19th century middle-class Americans, and the meanings it suggested — a proper, land-owning, civilized family — were not difficult to read. This "civilized" couple of 1890 (the woman seated with a parasol, the man with a walking stick) is contrasted with their 1830 predecessors, who are shown in the inset, reiterating the theme of progress through the use of mechanical farming equipment.

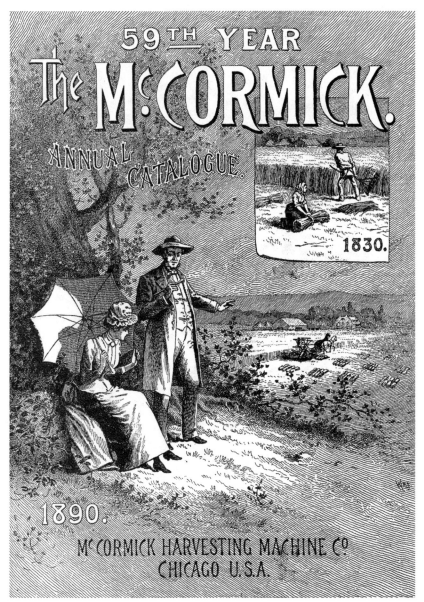

Figure 4.19   McCormick's 1890 catalog. (Wisconsin Historical Society, WHi-36508)

This message of progress is reinforced by the back cover — a full-color image showing the man of the house educating his children about the world (see Figure 4.20). Titled "Teaching Object Lesson" this image aligns the empire of McCormick (where McCormick is *king*) with a geography lesson about the civilized and soon to be civilized world.

Figure 4.20 "Teaching Object Lesson," back cover, McCormick's 1890 catalog. (Collection of the author)

Portrayed on a globe, a way of depicting the Earth that, as Denis Cosgrove tells us, induces "desires of ordering and controlling,"[10] the kingdom of McCormick *is* the known and ordered world, and vice versa. Just as the globe serves as an object lesson for the son in the image, teaching him a commercial geography, so too the image itself is an object lesson to those who see it. The family represents the highest ideals of civilized whiteness. They are depicted in a proper Victorian parlor, complete with potted palms, classical statues, learned books, ornate furniture, and lush carpets. This image also draws on a long artistic tradition that dates to the late 18th century — a tradition in both painting and photography of depicting women and children being taught a geography lesson by a patriarch.[11] Although many viewers of this catalog may not have been familiar with the details of this genre, the image itself was easy to read. The family is engaged in a geography lesson — learning about the ordered world through the modern techniques of surveying and mapping that were available in one's living room via an atlas or globe. The patriarch instructs his son about the commercial world ("My children on this globe you will see the harvest fields of the world where the McCormick is ever king"), while the daughter looks on. The image on the wall gives us a sense of what the purported civilized world looks like outside the parlor walls — the American yeoman farmer tending to his productive fields, atop his McCormick. The message is clear: agricultural machinery has brought civilization and prosperity to the American West, making possible the riches within the home parlor, and presumably making that prosperity possible around the globe. As the text from the 1891 catalog confirms, McCormick presented itself as the mechanism for promoting civilization wherever its machines were being used: "That the McCormick has been no unimportant factor in promoting civilization and developing the resources of the land, is recognized by all who watch history as it is making."

The 1893 Columbian Exposition in Chicago served as a perfect platform for McCormick Company to link its civilizing work in the United States to its new overseas role, given that the Exposition's stated purpose was to demonstrate to the world the progress of the United States since its "discovery" by Columbus 400 years before. The exhibits of American farm machinery that commanded a large section of Agriculture Hall at the Exposition centered on a large globe, around which revolved an array of modern farm machinery. The message of such a visual spectacle was not difficult to read; at just a quick glance, visitors could understand the global spread of American progress. As the largest manufacturer of farm equipment, and a company based in Chicago, McCormick made sure that its exhibit was a focal point within this visual spectacle. The company's exhibit centered on two working models or panoramas that depicted, with moving miniaturized parts, both the company's main manufacturing plant in Chicago and a McCormick binder at work in an agricultural field. To ensure that viewers recognized the company's newfound global reach, the company's promotional materials included catalogs and brochures that listed the places around the world where McCormick machines were being used to release the "farmer from the drudgery of life." In this way, McCormick Harvesting Machine Company, like its many competitors, promoted its products by elaborating how farm machinery was helping "other" peoples move forward on the hierarchy of civilization.

The model of the company's plant was, as a guidebook explained, "mechanically constructed to show the movement of railroad trains and lake vessels in and about the McCormick yards and warehouses."[12] In other words, spectators were offered a view of McCormick's manufacturing complex as if they were actually seeing it in operation from a stationary point high above the plant — a vision of constant motion and movement of goods and vehicles. The other side was similarly constructed to show the binding machine at work in agricultural fields. This novel form of exhibition — a double working model — was "constantly surrounded with crowds of admiring on-lookers," *Halligan's Illustrated World's Fair* commented.[13] Linking city and country, farming and industry, was not particularly unusual,[14] but the depiction of the actual movement of vehicles that made those links happen was. The display was a vivid depiction of modernity — of the precise and regularized movement through space that mechanization made possible.

And that movement through space was not limited to national borders. McCormick's 1893 catalog that was available at the Exposition made the international connection clear. At the top of each page of the catalog was a small horizontal image of a long train, with McCormick Light Steel Binders and Mowers written on it. Each image was captioned with the name of a different country or region where the McCormick was being sold: Brazil, France, Asia, Norway, Mexico, Ireland, Sweden, Turkey, Germany, Australia, Russia, Scotland, England, Siberia, Ecuador, Greece, Denmark, Hindoostan, India, Cuba, Spain, Egypt, Chile, Italy, Portugal, Canada, Uruguay, Wales, Roumania, New Zealand, Belgium, Victoria, Africa. In other words, the trains that visitors could view at the McCormick exhibit at the Fair, trains picking up products at the Chicago factory, were presumably headed not only for Nebraska and other domestic destinations but also these other, far more distant places. The catalog's opening text makes the point: "The sun does not shine on a grain-growing land where the McCormick is unknown, and to our farmer friends throughout this wide domain we here wish to renew all former pledges, and return again our sincerest thanks for your high appreciation of our efforts." Most Exposition commentators and guidebooks mentioned McCormick's international prominence: "So widespread is the distribution of this make of grain and grass harvesting machines that it has been well said: 'The sun never sets on the McCormick.'"[15]

McCormick's 1894 catalog returned to the familiar theme of American progress measured by the presence of the productive yeoman farmer. Its cover, for example, makes explicit the relationship between a white, patriarchal farmer and American nationalism (see Figure 4.21). As the text reads, the farmer (sitting atop the McCormick in the bottom image)

Figure 4.21 "The Farmer, Our Country's Defender ... ," front cover, McCormick's 1894 catalog. (Wisconsin Historical Society, WHi-4415)

is the key to national prosperity, to the "balance" of power, and the greatness of the nation. The back cover reiterates the importance of the yeoman to American identity through images that situate farmers centrally in the first skirmishes of the Revolutionary War in Concord and Lexington (see Figure 4.22). The inset image depicts the ride of Paul

Figure 4.22 "Honor to Whom Honor is Due," back cover, McCormick's 1894 catalog. (Wisconsin Historical Society, WHi-4416)

Revere, alerting farmers (one is shown out in the fields with his work animals and plow) to the "call to arms." The larger image depicts a battle scene at the edge of a farmstead (note the plow, barn, and haystacks), with British soldiers standing in formation in the open fields beyond. Taken together, these two covers present the farmer as the quintessential American hero.

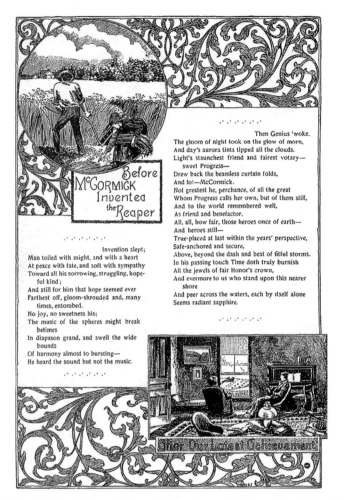

Figure 4.23 "Before McCormick Invented the Reaper," McCormick's 1894 catalog, 1. (Wisconsin Historical Society, WHi-5448)

On the first page of the catalog is a poem with accompanying images that depict life "before McCormick invented the reaper" and "after our latest achievement" (see Figure 4.23). Before the McCormick, women had to work in the fields, and men's agricultural work was laborious; these were "savage" times, "no joy, no sweetness his." After the McCormick, the patriarchal American pastoral is achieved, with machines working the productive fields, and husband and wife occupying the cultivated and civilized parlor, watching out the window as "sweet Progress drew back" the "curtain folds." So the McCormick makes possible civilization in the form of the American pastoral

— its mechanized form of farming brings prosperity to the nation at the same time that it allows for men to assume their civilized role of patriarch and women to tend to the domestic sphere. And just as McCormick machines had brought prosperity to American farmers, they could work in a similar way to bring wealth to other nations.

This, it seems, was the primary story being told by McCormick in the early 1890s, a story of progress that was narrated as follows: given that farm machinery had been a primary force in the prosperity of the United States, since it eliminated much of farmers' manual labor and also helped farmers make productive use of lands in the Great Plains, the export of American farm machinery to other parts of the world would bring similar benefits. Ultimately, then, McCormick machines would re-create American civilization — the yeoman presiding over his productive fields — in foreign lands. Although officially delivered at the Chicago Exposition, the ideas that formed Turner's frontier thesis had already been circulated and found their way into McCormick's and other farm machinery company's displays and catalogs.[16] In encountering and modifying wilderness, diverse immigrants had become American. Through the wonders of trains and shipping routes, the Americanization process was now happening in other lands throughout the world.

McCormick's 1897 catalog puts this imagery front and center, with a cover image called "The Ship of Progress" (see Figure 4.24). The image features a ship that is literally named "Progress"; sitting precariously at the ship's bow, under the McCormick flag, is an actual reaper, ready to be unloaded at the next shoreline. Destined for foreign lands, this steamship is, according to its accompanying poem, "plowing" ahead carrying "reaper freight" to "each wave-kissed shore" where a "welcome holds for thee." Other international companies — including many of the other farm machinery firms, such as Deering and Buckeye — also used nautical images to represent commercial and civilizational progress.[17] For example, H.J. Heinz Company repeatedly used the imagery of travels aboard a ship to show how their products were bringing civilization to the world (see Figure 4.25). For Heinz, as for McCormick, the emphasis is on a form of shipping that brings commercial trade and travelers, not weapons and soldiers, thus distinguishing the United States and the future from Europe and the past. The products carried on board were welcomed at the shoreline because they brought with them the benefits of progress.

The 1896 McCormick catalog cover image suggested what that welcome would be: McCormick machines being honored in a parade of nations, each represented by a man dressed in national costume

Figure 4.24 "The Ship of Progress," front cover, McCormick's 1897 catalog. (Wisconsin Historical Society, WHi-4419)

Figure 4.25 "The 57 Varieties across Seas." (*The 57*, anniversary issue (1909): 21. Courtesy of H.J. Heinz Company)

Figure 4.26   "Triumphant throughout All Nations," front cover, McCormick's 1896 catalog. (Wisconsin Historical Society, WHi-4418)

holding the flag of his country (see Figure 4.26). The United States is depicted in similar form, with the first man in the lineup holding an American flag and Uncle Sam riding atop the first reaper, saluting the crowd with his outstretched hat. Resembling in some ways a military parade, complete with flags and salutes, the image suggests a peaceful "triumph," one brought about by farm machinery instead of cannon fire. Uncle Sam is "triumphant throughout all nations," not by military strength but by industrial power. The back cover image makes this link apparent (see Figure 4.27). Here, we see the vast McCormick plant in Chicago producing (notice the billowing smoke) and shipping out its machines by train and ship; this scene is grouped with an image of a farmer using a McCormick mower, alongside the parade of nations. Here, as in all McCormick ads, industry and agriculture are seen as twinned activities that have created American power and the ability to bring progress to the world.

Harvesting the World

By 1900, McCormick's advertising could rightly boast that the company's products were being shipped worldwide. Maintaining the use

Figure 4.27 "McCormick Reaper Works," back cover, McCormick's 1896 catalog. (Wisconsin Historical Society, WHi-36509)

of the word "triumph" in its title ("The End of the Century Witnesses the Triumphs of the McCormick"), but never directly referring to the wars of 1898, the catalog uses the motif of the end of the century to list humankind's accomplishments, of course, placing the McCormick reaper at the top of the list: "The chief agent, the chief initiator, and the chief instigator, the great source, the fountain-head of this wonderful progress of the century is the McCormick, for without the McCormick the illimitable wheat fields, the bread-bearing areas of the world would have remained as of yore beyond the grasp of man." The invention of the McCormick reaper is placed center stage in the economic development of the world, with no national borders mentioned, a world divided into grain and grass growing regions, not states: "The McCormick for the first time in history made bread cheap in the temperate regions — cheap and constant. The McCormick banished the fear of our fathers — famine times — the fear of the failure of the harvest. This glorious invention has doubled the food resources of all nations. It has made possible The Agricultural Capture of the World's Grain and Grass."

At the same time, the company produced a different kind of advertising brochure — a photographic "album" showing people harvesting grain in different regions and countries around the world. Titled "100 Harvesting Scenes All around the World," the booklet literally contained that, 100 black-and-white photographs depicting people using different types of tools and machinery to harvest and mow grasses and grains. The text of this booklet was in three languages: English, French, and German. McCormick was long in the habit of publishing its catalogs in several languages; however, this booklet was unique in that it contained side-by-side translations. Part of the reason for this is that the booklet was given out at the 1900 Paris World's Exposition and was therefore meant for a European audience. In any case, the appearance of multiple languages in the booklet added a decidedly international flavor to this corporate advertisement.

The use of photographs (made possible by new printing technologies) was certainly novel and lent a documentary quality to the booklet, as if it was simply recording a series of "facts" about the world. In addition, each image was linked to the others through its formal presentation — its decorative border and standardized form of captioning (see Figure 4.28 to 4.30), similar to Singer's many sets of nation cards. The result was a document that appeared more as a geography textbook than as an advertising tool, but this textbook was not organized regionally, as would have been common at the time. In fact, the images are arranged in a rather haphazard fashion, with, for example, an image of harvesting in Mexico positioned between France and Russia. The key distinction within this group of photos was between those that showed people using modern machinery and those that depicted people *not* using machinery. This distinction, however, is never marked explicitly as such — the photos are not grouped accordingly, nor are the methods distinguished from each other in terms of calling the former "modern" and the latter "primitive." The photos are simply labeled with the activity happening in that image, such as "Reaping with knives in Central India" or "A farm scene in Columbia City, Indiana, USA," or "Harvest scene in South Eastern Russia. The McCormick Daisy Reaper." What separates India from Russia, for example, is the use or lack of use of machinery, not any intrinsic difference of character or culture. In other words, the category of difference that matters is the consumption and use of McCormick machinery, not race or culture.

In its 1900 catalog, the company put this sentiment into words in this quote about its new rice-harvester machine:

The prosperity and progress of the farming world are bounded by the use of McCormick machines. The reaper, invented by Cyrus H. McCormick in 1830, released from agriculture

Figure 4.28 "The McCormick Right Hand Binder in Mexico," *100 Harvesting Scenes All around the World,* McCormick adverstising booklet, 1900. (Wisconsin Historical Society, WHi-5443)

Figure 4.29 "Reaping with Knives in Central India," *100 Harvesting Scenes All around the World,* McCormick adverstising booklet, 1900. (Wisconsin Historical Society, WHi-5445)

La Lieuse à Main Droite McCormick dans les Steppes de la Russie.
Der McCormick rechtsschneidende Binder in den Steppen Rußlands.
The McCormick Right Hand Binder on the Steppes in Russia.

Figure 4.30   "The McCormick Right Hand Binder on the Steppes in Russia," *100 Harvesting Scenes All around the World,* McCormick adverstising booklet, 1900. (Wisconsin Historical Society, WHi-36510)

the labor necessary for the developments of our mining and manufacturing industries, from which the great commercial wealth of the white races has sprung. The commerce of the progressive nations has multiplied in proportion to their use of reaping machinery. The unprogressive nations are those that have no machinery to gather their food products. China, India and other rice-eating nations have remained stagnant during the marvelous progress of the white races, not because their people eat rice, but because their methods of producing it are so slow and laborious that all their energies are absorbed in obtaining food.

As this quote makes clear, McCormick presented an image of the world in which countries and peoples are distinguished from each other by their use of technology, not by their races or cultures. As Michael Adas has shown, using technology as the "measure of man" was a common rhetorical mode of dominance in both the British colonial regimes and American commercial empires.[18] At the turn of the century, the railway was the most powerful technological symbol of Western dominance. In Adas's words, "more than any other technological innovation, the railway embodied the great material advances associated with the first Industrial Revolution and dramatized the gap which that process had created between the Europeans and all non-Western peoples."[19] McCormick Harvesting Machine Company, as we have seen, continually mentioned in its list of great inventions the railway first, followed by the steamship, and then of course the reaper. In this way, the McCormick reaper became associated with the great machines of Western civilization. Yet unlike the railway and steamship, the reaper was a machine meant for use by "natives." The images and words in McCormick's catalogs all depict foreign peoples using the machines in their own countries, actively bringing the benefits of technology themselves, but with Western help. Again, the dominant message is that the consumption and use of technology would transform culture and place, just as the American wilderness had been transformed into the garden, in the process creating the "true" American.

These themes of transformation through the use of the McCormick, the reiteration of the frontier thesis in foreign lands, continued as the dominant motif of McCormick advertising throughout the first decade of the 20th century. The merger of McCormick with four of its competitors in 1902 — forming IH — did little to alter advertising schemas. Each of the five companies continued to issue advertising under their own names, while IH was slowly introduced as its own mark. McCormick was the largest of the companies when they merged, and it maintained control over IH and its advertising and promotion. The various images that formed the 1900 McCormick "harvest scenes" booklet were reprinted in color and circulated as IH postcards in 1909 and 1910 (see Figure 4.31 and 4.32). With the series title, "Harvest Scenes around the World," printed on the back, these cards circulated widely through American homes, spreading the message of the dominance of IH in international fields and its role in helping different peoples harvest their grain and feed their population. The South America card, for example, depicted a harvester in action being pulled by oxen (see Figure 4.33), with the following caption: "South America — modern harvesting machines on the wide pampas in the Argentine Republic. A new agricultural empire, which promises soon to rank next to the U.S. as a wheat producer." Argentina's future is presented as limitless as the horizon on the image — about to become modern and American with the use of American products.

By 1909, this sort of message had become normalized. The United States made technological products that were "normally" being sold overseas, and by using them, other nations were on their way to modernity, if not already there. The message had been repeated so many times and in so many ways, that it need not even be commented

SIBERIA—A HARVEST SCENE ON THE TUNDRA OF TOBOLSK WHERE AMERICAN HARVESTING
MACHINES ARE GRADUALLY WORKING THEIR WAY INTO FAVOR.

Figure 4.31 "Siberia," International Harvester advertising postcard, 1909. (Collection of the author)

UNITED STATES—IN THE LAND OF SUNSHINE AND PLENTY, HARVESTING, LIKE ALL OTHER THINGS,
IS DONE ON A LARGE SCALE, AND MACHINES CUTTING A WIDE SWATH ARE NECESSARY.

Figure 4.32 "United States," International Harvester advertising postcard, 1909. (Collection of the author)

upon. On one South American postcard, a woman named Amelia wrote to another women living in the same town of Verona, New York (see Figure 4.34): "Dear Hattie, I don't know whether I can finish that piece or not ... my point doesn't work good. I tried it Thurs-

SOUTH AMERICA—MODERN HARVESTING MACHINES ON THE WIDE PAMPAS IN THE ARGENTINE REPUBLIC, *
NEW AGRICULTURAL EMPIRE. WHICH PROMISES SOON TO RANK NEXT TO THE U. S. AS A WHEAT PRODUCER.

Figure 4.33 "South America," International Harvester advertising postcard, 1909. (Collection of the author)

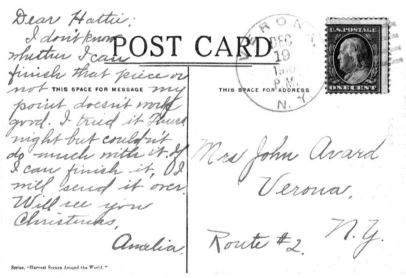

Figure 4.34 Back of "South America" postcard, 1909. (Collection of the author)

day night but couldn't do much with it. I will send it over. Will see you Christmas." Dated December 19, 1910, this card was being used as a relatively cheap form of communication (the stamp cost 1 cent) between two women living in upstate New York, carrying messages about sewing and perhaps some information about Argentina. The international and the domestic were joined together here, a "cosmopolitan domesticity," in the words of Kristin Hoganson,[20] but a cosmopolitanism that was so mundane as to not require attention.

McCormick/IH's stories about foreign peoples and foreign lands produced and were constituted through a set of common narratives about progress and place. The frontier narrative was the most persistent, a depiction of harvesting machines in action turning wilderness into gardens and savages into modern peoples. In the 1909 set of postcards depicting harvest scenes around the world, only India was shown still using "primitive" tools; the rest of the world had become modern by using harvesting machines. American technology was presented as the key to economic development and cultural progress. The yeoman farmer, the linchpin of American democracy and economic success, was now sitting atop harvesters and reapers and mowers in many regions of the world. IH represented its commercial empire as a series of American gardens, producing food for the nations and creating consumers for American products. When Amelia sent her postcard to Hattie, she probably did not notice the image of Argentina on the front, partly because it was so similar to images of the United States. It was as natural for Argentine farmers to be using IH harvesters as it was for American farmers. By 1909, McCormick harvesters had successfully transformed foreign farmers into American yeoman, though yeoman who lived outside American borders.

Endnotes

1. Richard White, "Frederick Jackson Turner and Buffalo Bill," *The Frontier in American Culture,* ed. James R. Grossman (Berkeley: University of California Press, 1994).
2. Ibid., 17.
3. For a more full exposition of the origins and significances of the imagery of the yeoman and the garden, see Henry Nash Smith, *Virgin Land: The American West as Symbol and Myth* (New York: Vintage Books, 1950) and Leo Marx, *The Machine in the Garden: Technology and the Pastoral Ideal in America* (New York: Oxford University Press, 1964).
4. Anne McClintock, *Imperial Leather: Race, Gender, and Sexuality in the Colonial Contest* (New York: Routledge, 1995).
5. Ibid., 37.
6. Raymond Williams, *Keywords: A Vocabulary of Culture and Society* (New York: Oxford University Press, 1985).
7. White (1994), 15.

8. See, for example, Richard Slotkin, *The Fatal Environment: The Myth of the Frontier in the Age of Industrialization, 1800–1890* (Norman: University of Oklahoma Press, 1985); Richard Slotkin, *Regeneration through Violence: The Mythology of the American Frontier, 1600–1860* (Norman: University of Oklahoma Press, 2000); Philip Joseph Deloria, Playing Indian (New Haven, CT: Yale University Press, 1998); Susan Scheckel, *The Insistence of the Indian: Race and Nationalism in Nineteenth-Century American Culture* (Princeton, NJ: Princeton University Press, 1998); and Mark David Spence, *Dispossessing the Wilderness: Indian Removal and the Making of the National Parks* (New York: Oxford University Press, 1999).

9. See John Berger, *Ways of Seeing* (New York: Penguin Books, 1995) and Stephen Daniels, *Fields of Vision: Landscape Imagery and National Identity in England and the United States* (Cambridge, UK: Polity Press, 1993).

10. Denis Cosgrove, *Apollo's Eye: A Cartographic Genealogy of the Earth in the Western Imagination* (Baltimore, MD: Johns Hopkins University Press, 2001), 5.

11. Joan M. Schwartz, "The Geography Lesson: Photographs and the Construction of Imaginative Geographies," *Journal of Historical Geography*, 22, 1 (1996): 16–45.

12. *World's Columbian Exposition Illustrated* (Chicago: J.B. Campbell, 1893), 156.

13. "McCormick's Splendid Exhibit," *Halligan's Illustrated World's Fair*, 5 (September 1893), 643.

14. William Cronon's masterful book *Nature's Metropolis: Chicago and the Great West* (New York: W.W. Norton, 1991) makes clear the material and metaphoric connections between Chicago and its hinterland.

15. John J. Flinn, *The Standard Guide to Chicago, Illustrated*, World's Fair edition (Chicago: The Standard Guide Co., 1893), 527.

16. For example, Deering's promotional brochure at the Fair titled "Triumphs of the 19th Century" drew on similar themes. According to Deering's advertising campaign, the United States itself was the greatest of these "triumphs" — "The United States of America has been the theater of the greatest advancement of this century of progress" — and this advancement has been made possible by the farmer, the "bone and sinew of the nation." American farmers helped achieve this end by populating the West, breathing "free air" and producing "wholesome, nourishing food." Together with Deering farm machines, American farmers produced American greatness: "It was not until the great West was filled up with bravehearted, strong-bodied farmers that the country achieved its present eminence." In its pamphlet called "The Moment of Triumph," Buckeye Mower and Reaper Company billed itself as the maker of implements of peace, and used this rhetoric to position America (and the company) as the pinnacle of civilization, an improved-upon version

of Roman greatness: "It was an interesting custom, in the zenith of Rome's greatness, to erect a triumphal arch to celebrate a victory, or to add additional lustre to the commemoration of the military exploits of a victorious general.... With the advance of civilization ruthless war has succumbed to the quietness of peace. Spears have been beaten into pruning hooks and chariots of destruction turned into harvesting machines. 'Peace hath her victories no less than war,' and erected in the hearts and minds of the agriculturists of the civilized world of to-day is a triumphal arch to the Buckeye as the 'World's Conqueror.'"

17. For example, Buckeye's 1892 advertising brochure used the shipping motif to represent the company's progress in bringing civilization to America and elsewhere.

18. Michael Adas, *Machines as the Measure of Men: Science, Technology, and Ideologies of Western Dominance* (Ithaca, NY: Cornell University Press, 1989).

19. Ibid., 221.

20. Kristin Hoganson, "Cosmopolitan Domesticity: Importing the American Dream, 1865–1921," *American Historical Review,* 107 (2002): 55–83.

5

Holidays with Heinz:
The Foreign Travels of
Purity and Pickles

Through samples, carried sometimes by our own representatives and at others by "globe trotters" from the great commission houses of London and New York; sometimes by missionaries or tourists, and frequently by means we are unable to trace, our products have found their way, literally to the ends of the earth, and we claim with justifiable pride that the name of "Heinz" has become known in every country and to every nation of the world.
— *Pickles*, 6, 6, (1902): 2

Railways, which play such an important part in the development of any country, are being projected in all directions throughout China, and the shriek of the locomotive whistle is to-day heard in places where only ten years ago an European was hardly heard of and never seen. If you are curious to see the China of opium smokers, dried rats, and women of small feet, you must make haste, for such things will be among the vanished customs and curiosities of the country twenty years hence.
— Alexander MacWillie, "Impressions of the Orient," *The 57 Life*, 3, 2, (1907): 4–5

When H.J. Heinz Company began selling its manufactured food products overseas in the last decades of the 19th century, it did little to alter its sales and advertising strategies that had proved so successful within the United States. Sales agents were dispersed to the emerging markets in Africa, East Asia, and Europe, making visits to local groceries with their samples of Heinz products and dispensing advertising cards and posters. Yet, as the first quote above (taken from Heinz's newsletter) makes clear, the company suggested other means by which their products reached the shelves of stores overseas; globe trotters, missionaries, and tourists, the company claimed, were also responsible for the diffusion of their products "to the ends of the earth." These travelers, apparently, were unintentionally spreading the "word" about Heinz by leaving sample products behind during their trips. Heinz Company, in other words, represented its international experiences as little more than overseas travels by at times unsuspecting agents of transmission.

This discursive disassociation of the company from its marketing efforts runs counter to the huge material investments in transportation, refrigeration, advertising, and personnel that made those international sales possible. Yet this self-presentation of the company's efforts overseas as little more than extensions of holiday visits created a very nonthreatening vision of the company's expansion. It also created a "touristic" and nonthreatening image of other cultures and places — an image of foreign countries and cultures that, although exotic, were soon to become familiar. As one of Heinz's salesmen, Alexander MacWillie, wrote about China, its exotic qualities "will be among the vanished customs and curiosities of the country twenty years hence." Taken together, these quotes from Heinz's newsletters suggest that the company was intent on creating a domesticated vision of its international experiences: through travels and visits, Heinz products were being brought to foreign countries and customers, whose exotic customs were vanishing, to be replaced by familiar, domestic visions. In other words, Heinz's international marketing efforts were presented — both within its public advertising and its own internal newsletter — not as business ventures per se, but as social visits and holidays, and foreign peoples and places were depicted as potential hosts.

This domesticated corporate vision was not new for Heinz. From the 1880s on, Heinz Company represented itself as a patriarchal family and its expansive sales force as no more than travelers. However, when the company began in earnest to market its goods overseas, this new internationalism presented a challenge to the company's domestic vision. How and why this challenge was met and the effects of this discursive fashioning of foreign customers and countries into familiar, almost familial, relationships is the subject of this chapter.

The Pure Heinz Family

When the U.S. government passed the Pure Food and Drug Act of 1906, which regulated food additives and mandated labeling of product ingredients, they did so with the ardent support of the leading food manufacturing firms of the time. Government regulation assuaged the public's fear of adulterated food and gave large companies legitimacy and a competitive edge over smaller, cost-cutting food companies who often used additives.[1] Heinz Company's founder and president, Henry J. Heinz, spearheaded the public campaign to enact these federal regulations and initiated some of the behind-the-scenes political maneuverings that were finally necessary to convince President Theodore Roosevelt to support laws that intervened in the workings of private business. For Heinz, an experienced businessman keenly aware of "modern" business strategies, such a strong public association of his company with the new laws served to consolidate his company's reputation as a manufacturer of pure, and therefore good, food. The company wasted no time in exploiting this association; a 1906 advertisement that appeared in *Munsey's Magazine* stated, "Heinz Products are made not only to conform to but actually exceed the requirements of all State and National Pure Food Laws" (see Figure 5.1).

Heinz, of course, was not alone in supporting pure food legislation or aligning his products with the benefits of purity. The pure food "scare" of the early 1900s initially focused on the quality of meat, as Upton Sinclair's *The Jungle* rallied popular protest against the less-than-sanitary conditions within meatpacking plants. Although at first measuring federal legislation as a setback to business, the big five meatpacking companies eventually recognized the advantages of an inspection system that guaranteed the quality of their products, particularly, as Levenstein argues, a system that was "government-financed, government-run."[2] Heinz's direct competitors in food processing, Campbell's and Franco-American, were also won over by the benefits of federal regulatory legislation. But Heinz Company was unique in its early and deep-seated commitment to two modern business practices: it relied on mass advertising and promotional campaigns to gain a competitive edge, and it worked toward creating an international business network, buying raw materials and selling manufactured foods throughout the world. Through that mass advertising, Heinz created an image of itself that aligned the company and its products to the related notions of purity and family — both notions working together to suggest products that were uncontaminated, either by chemical or moral agents. This first section, therefore, outlines how and why this association with purity

HEINZ

Sunshine
and
Purity

Sunshine, fresh air, immaculate cleanliness and perfect sanitation—these are the conditions that prevail to the farthest corners of the Heinz Kitchens.

The doors are wide open—always have been. Last year we had 30,000 visitors, and they are still coming in ever-increasing numbers to marvel at the thoroughness with which the home of the "Girl in the White Cap" is conducted.

There is nothing that thought can suggest to make surroundings more conducive to cleaner work—to purer, better food.

Most important of all—Heinz products are made not only to conform to but actually exceed the requirements of all State and National Pure Food Laws.

HEINZ
Tomato Ketchup

Ketchup is a product frequently adulterated and colored. Heinz Tomato Ketchup is absolutely pure. It is made of choice, fresh, ripe tomatoes and pure spices, bottled hot from the kettle and is thoroughly sterilized. Get a bottle from your grocer.

Let us send you a copy of our booklet, "The Spice of Life."

57
VARIETIES

H. J. HEINZ COMPANY,

New York   Pittsburgh   Chicago   London

In answering this advertisement it is desirable that you mention MUNSEY'S MAGAZINE.

Figure 5.1   "Heinz, Sunshine and Purity," Heinz advertisement from *Munsey's Magazine,* 1906. (Library and Archives Division, Historical Society of Western Pennsylvania, Pittsburgh, PA)

and family was fashioned, as this is critical to understanding why Heinz represented foreign countries and consumers as members of the American "family."

"Our market is the world," declared Henry J. Heinz, founder of Heinz foods, in 1886, after the company's first overseas sale.[3] By 1900, Heinz sold over 200 (not 57!) products throughout the world, making it the first and largest promoter of American food products overseas. The technologies of preserving, bottling, and canning food items (beans, relishes, pickles, jams, jellies, and other condiments), developed throughout the latter half of the 19th century, were fully exploited by Henry Heinz, as he moved his company from a small, bottling enterprise in 1869 to one of the country's largest and most profitable businesses by 1900.[4] According to company historian Robert Alberts, at the turn of the century, H.J. Heinz Company operated, in addition to its huge factory in Pittsburgh, "nine branch factories in six states, 38 salting houses in nine states, a branch house in London, and agencies around the world."[5]

Heinz's success was partly due to its exploitation of a new market created by substituting products made in factories for those traditionally produced at home by women. Similar to the burgeoning textile and clothing industries, the food manufacturing business depended on reshaping women's subjectivities from producers of goods to consumers. Through aggressive advertising, Heinz, along with other manufacturers, hoped to convince middle-class women that buying packaged food was as good as, and often better than, what they made at home. According to Levenstein, the popularization of the idea that manufactured food was "good" food, and therefore better than what had preceded it, began with the mass-marketing of ready-to-eat breakfast cereals.[6] The two dominant companies — Kellogg's and Post— aligned their products with health and hygiene and spent large sums of money to advertise and promote these linkages. The tactics these companies pursued in promoting their new products served as important lessons for other food manufacturing companies: link your product to abstract qualities considered desirable by middle-class Americans, and advertise those linkages aggressively. In addition, given that there was little in the way of taste or quality to distinguish between most mass-produced food products (the standardization of technologies of food manufacturing led to uniform products), the only way to distinguish, for example, one type of cornflake from the other, was the development and promotion of brand names. This, as Levenstein argues, certainly "put a premium on advertising."[7] According to the records of the N.W. Ayer Advertising Agency, the largest in the country, in 1877, advertisements for food accounted for less than 1% of its business; by 1901, that number had risen to almost 15%, and food products "remained the single most advertised class of commodity until the 1930s."[8] Most of these advertisements were aimed at middle-class women, convincing them to purchase healthier and more convenient packaged foods to substitute for those "less modern" items they had previously made at home.

However, again like the textile and clothing industries, food manufacturing was extremely labor intensive and relied on hiring women at low wages. Heinz employed girls and women in almost all aspects of food production — from peeling and skinning to bottling and washing. And they were paid significantly less than men; for example, in 1888, immigrant girls starting at Heinz were paid 5 cents an hour, about $3 a week, whereas male unskilled mill hands were paid 15 cents an hour, three times as much.[9] Heinz, of course, was not alone in relying on women, often immigrant, laborers. As Goodman and Redclift argue, the food manufacturing business has been characterized from the beginning by its reliance on the inexpensive labor of women.[10] To attain and maintain profit margins, therefore, textile and food manufacturing businesses relied on women as producers *and* as consumers.

Yet this dual role for women — working-class women as producers and middle-class women as consumers — contradicted the reigning ideology of separate spheres. Positioning women as consumers and men as producers kept separate and complementary the two value systems necessary to keep industrial America functioning: a commitment to hard work and diligence and, at the same time, a willingness to give in to desire and indulge in material goods. Despite the realities of women's lives as laborers, ideological constraints deemed the feminine subject to be a consuming one. For the most part, manufacturers were not particularly bothered by this apparent contradiction between a reality of women laborers and the ideology of women as consumers. As with many other types of capitalist endeavors, the conditions of production — that is, women factory workers — were simply hidden or obscured, literally removed from view and from the flow of ideas and images that proliferated in Victorian advertising and material culture.

However, food manufacturing was different: the actual processes of food production were of interest to those buying the products. It is not difficult to understand why. As is still true today, how food is made is important to consumers.[11] Unlike, for example, textiles, food is a commodity that is ingested, literally taken into the body. Its quality, and by implication the conditions of its production, are constantly under scrutiny for signs of contamination. This was particularly true at the turn of the century, when manufactured food was new to consumers, and no federal regulations controlled its production. As a result, Heinz Company found it particularly useful to display, as if on exhibit, the processes of production in its plant and the labor that made it possible, particularly the labor of women. The company did so in two ways: first, it literally put its business on display, becoming the first manufacturer to open its factory to plant tours for the public; second, it used images of the factory and its women workers as advertisements for the company, saturating popular magazines with depictions of pure, clean women workers producing packaged foods in clean and orderly surroundings.

Yet, by doing so, Heinz and other food companies made visible their women laborers — something that threatened the ideology that aligned women as consumers and men as producers. It was important, therefore, to position women workers as feminine subjects, little different from their middle-class, consuming sisters. This reinforced Heinz Company's representation of itself as a family working together toward a common goal, not laborers working for a wage. In order to represent its women workers as bourgeois daughters and sisters, Heinz situated them in feminine spaces, discursively fashioning its factory into a home. For example, the production areas were presented as model kitchens, lunchrooms became dining rooms, and outdoor spaces were transformed into gardens. These representations were reinforced, both on the tours that were given through the plant and in the advertising campaigns. In 1906, 10 years after Heinz's "model" plant buildings were constructed across the Allegheny from Pittsburgh, the company's newsletter reported that a record-breaking number of 25,000 visitors had toured the plant that year: "Instead of resting content with the announcement that their goods are pure and clean," Heinz Company, which does "not believe in closed doors," took "visitors through their plant from top to bottom and let them see the conditions existing for themselves."[12] Those visitors were first led into a reception room, lavishly decorated with oil paintings from Heinz's personal collection, palm trees, and displays of Heinz products, before proceeding into the "model kitchens" (the processing rooms), the bottling rooms, and then to the sections of the factory complex not directly related to production. The girls' dining hall, a large lunch room for women workers that was completed in 1897, apparently was a highlight of the tour and became a cornerstone of Heinz propaganda, as it served to reinforce the image of the company as benevolent and of its workers as "proper" women. According to the company's newsletter, visitors to the girls' new dining hall "are wont to linger, impressed by its comfort and beauty."[13] Like the reception room, the long hall was decorated with paintings from Heinz's collection and was ventilated with windows along both sides, creating a scene that "arrests the visitor's attention and invites his admiration" while in the presence of things that "appeal to the sense of refinement and culture."[14]

Later that year, a roof garden for the girls was completed, allowing them to ascend the stairway from the dining hall and socialize after lunch on the benches or around the fountain. This roof garden was added to the tours. When a Pan-American delegation of businessmen toured the plant in 1897, "they were conveyed by an elevator to the roof garden," where they "lingered among the spreading palms

Figure 5.2   "Visitors' Sampling Room," Heinz trade card, circa 1895. (Warshaw Collection of Business Americana, Archives Center, National Museum of American History, Behring Center, Smithsonian Institution)

and bright hued flowers, which may have faintly suggested the flowery clime of their far away homes."[15] After being served refreshments, the delegates toured the dining hall while the girls were having lunch. It apparently was an "inspiring scene, and so different from anything else that the visitors had been shown elsewhere, that their words of surprise and appreciation were by no mean stinted."[16] The assumption of course is that Heinz treated his workers differently than other employers did, supplying them with spaces for leisure as well as work and creating an atmosphere more like a home than a factory.[17] In this way, women in the spaces of production did not necessarily disturb the reigning gender ideology; they worked, but within spaces little different from their home kitchens. As will be made clearer in the next section, this skillful representation of itself as a familial, not commercial, enterprise was put to good use when Heinz depicted its overseas expansion as part of a domestic, civilizing mission.

This blurring of the distinctions between working spaces and living spaces was carried through in Heinz's advertising. For example, in a promotional image from the late 1890s that appeared on a trade card and later on postcards (see Figure 5.2), distinguishing between the women who work and the women who consume is difficult. The packing room and the display room are represented in similar ways, with the same colors and general style of decor, creating spaces suitable for bourgeois women. Similarly, depictions of the roof garden (see Figure 5.3) used by Heinz for advertising present the space as

Figure 5.3   "One of the Roof Gardens," Heinz trade card, circa 1895. (Warshaw Collection of Business Americana, Archives Center, National Museum of American History, Behring Center, Smithsonian Institution)

completely feminized; with its potted palms, park benches, and outdoors sculptures, it appears little different from the Victorian house gardens that were considered a quintessential feminine space. The women are engaged in leisurely activities, such as strolling, chatting, and reading, conducting cultural affairs in an appropriately feminine setting. Again, the message is that these women are not "workers" of Heinz but are a part of its family; according to the inset image, they are "one of 'the 57' girls," as ornamental and beautiful as the multicolored jars of pickled food they hold.

Presented in such a way, women laborers introduced no threat to gender ideology. But they did do, in Mary Poovey's words, a lot of "ideological work."[18] The key to understanding this "work" is to explore the concept of purity. Given that the conditions of making food were of utmost importance to turn-of-the-century consumers, who were concerned about the quality of the new processed food they saw in their corner markets and on the pages of their magazines, H.J. Heinz Company made the term "purity" a hallmark of its promotional campaigns — the word appeared in almost every Heinz ad. The slogans "Heinz Sunshine and Purity," "Heinz 57 Varieties of Pure Food Products," and "Heinz Pure Vinegars" were repeated over and over in these advertisements in popular magazines, on the labels of products, and on signs painted on buildings and plastered on the sides of streetcars and inside subways. These advertising campaigns sought to make the term "purity" synonymous with the brand name Heinz.

But, as food historian Sidney Mintz reminds us, the term "purity" has two quite different, almost contradictory, meanings: on the one hand, it means simple, natural, free from human manipulation, and on the other hand, it means scientifically germ-free, antiseptic, completely manipulated.[19] Both meanings of the word were important to promoters of manufactured food products. Packaged food certainly had to be presented to consumers as germ-free and therefore safe to eat. For Heinz and other food manufacturers, this concern over the potential risks from eating processed food could be dealt with by assuring the public that their products were made germ-free from the rigorous application of modern science to the domestic "arts." A 1905 ad declares, "Everything that labor, thought and modern equipment can do is done to hold to that standard of excellence which characterizes Heinz Products." Yet this association to science and laboratory conditions was not necessarily conducive to selling food products; manufactured food was meant to be more convenient and perhaps more sanitary than what was made at home, but it certainly was not going to be bought if it was presented as qualitatively different from home-cooking. Manufactured food products, then, were meant to appear little different from what Mom made in her kitchen — they were just as wholesome and natural. A 1906 ad states that the "Heinz Way of preparing food products" was the result of "sound, healthy, natural developments," and a later (1924) advertising campaign focused on "The Homelike Kitchens of Heinz."

Heinz's presentation of a "feminized" workspace and workers contained both these meanings of purity. Because Victorian women were thought to be "naturally" pure and were considered the "natural" preparers of food, their presence in the workplace assured consumers that the food products were just as natural as what was made at home. Yet these women were also scrupulously clean, white, and scientifically germ-free. So both meanings of purity were promoted, without any apparent contradiction. A 1908 ad that appeared in Good Housekeeping made clear how these two meanings of purity, germ-free and natural, were embodied in the figure of a feminized women worker (see Figure 5.4). Titled "The Girl in the White Cap," the text of the ad reads: "In the spacious, finely-lighted, perfectly-ventilated Heinz Kitchens many hundreds of these neat, tidy, cheerful workers, daintily uniformed in aprons and caps of snowy white, co-operate with marvelously efficient methods and equipment in preparing pure food for the finest homes in the land." The workplace is not a factory but a "kitchen"; the workers are not rough and tumble working-class men but are naturally pure women, and therefore the products are both natural and scientifically germ-free.

FOOD PRODUCTS 107

The Girl in the White Cap

*Every housewife should be acquainted
with the Girl in the White Cap and her
painstaking work in the Home of the 57.*

In the spacious, finely-lighted, perfectly-ventilated
Heinz Kitchens many hundreds of these neat, tidy,
cheerful workers, daintily uniformed in aprons and caps
of snowy white, co-operate with marvelously efficient
methods and equipment in preparing pure food for
the finest homes in the land. Why not let the Heinz
Kitchen be *your* kitchen—and thus save a vast amount
of work and worry in setting your table, at the same time
retaining every quality of cleanliness, purity and home-
made goodness. This is what is offered in each of the

Each year we welcome 25,000 visitors who come
on all days and at all hours to marvel at the thoroughness, the precision, the care that attends every detail of
the Heinz Way of doing things. Can you come? If
not, let us send our beautiful booklet, "The Spice of
Life," picturing and describing the largest pure-food
kitchens in the world.

Your grocer sells Heinz products. Acquaint your-
self with them by trying the delicious Baked Beans
(three kinds), Fruit Preserves, Sweet Pickles, India
Relish, Tomato Chutney, Ketchup, etc.

H. J. HEINZ COMPANY, Pittsburgh, U. S. A.

Figure 5.4   "The Girl in the White Cap," Heinz advertisement from *Good Housekeeping,
1908.* (Collection of the author)

Other ideological "work" was being performed here as well. Purity is also about whiteness. Whiteness in food manufacturing correlates directly of course to cleanliness and, as Anne McClintock tells us, the obsession with cleanliness and its association to whiteness was invented along with and through imperialism, as a way of regulating, or distinguishing between those "contaminated" and those not, both at home and abroad.[20] In McClintock's words, to be clean and white in Victorian Britain meant that one had withstood "the fetid effluvia of the slums, the belching smoke of industry, social agitation, economic upheaval" and restored the "imperial body politic and the race."[21] To be clean and white in turn-of-the-century Pittsburgh was a feat of equal rigor. Commonly referred to as the "Smoky City," Pittsburgh was home to the largest steel and iron manufacturing plants in the country, to densely populated immigrant enclaves, and was the site of ongoing labor disputes, including one of the most notorious and bloodiest, the strike at the Carnegie Plant just outside Pittsburgh in Homestead, PA, where in 1892, Henry Clay Frick gave the order to Pinkerton Guards to shoot on the strikers, resulting in the deaths of 11 strikers and spectators and 7 guards. These conditions were not unique to Pittsburgh, of course. During the economic depressions of 1892 to 1897, strikes and disputes were widespread in the United States. Federal troops were called out in the Pullman strike in Chicago in 1894, and in the same year, 20,000 unemployed men marched on Washington, D.C. The end of this series of economic depressions coincided with the Spanish-American and the Philippine-American Wars, resulting in the first formal American imperialism.

In the midst of this economic, social, and geopolitical turmoil, Heinz Company captured an internal and then external informal empire by promoting its pure food made in pure conditions, untainted with contaminants. Heinz products and the company stood firm, apparently untouched by the threats posed by labor unrest and poor working conditions. To keep its workers content, Heinz created what would today be called a company "culture" that espoused the benefits of treating employees as members of a family. Dubbed "The Spirit of the 57" in the company newsletter, Heinz's philosophy recapitulated the tenets of corporate paternalism. After spotlighting the completion in 1900 of the company's auditorium, built to accommodate cultural events for the workers, the company's newsletter quotes Mr. Heinz's response as to whether money spent on the buildings was a good investment: "I have never thought of that. When we see that our employees lives are made happier and better we are fully repaid."[22] Unsaid but implied is that these "happy" workers are far less likely to demand better pay, join unions, or strike. Indeed, Heinz Company experienced none of the labor problems of its Pittsburgh neighbors, the steel and iron industries.

Heinz's "Spirit of the 57" — that is, happy and "fulfilled" workers — not only helped maintain a certain corporate "ethos" that kept at least some workers content with their jobs, it also was used to sell products, both at home and overseas. Food made under conditions considered "good" was potentially more desirable to consumers. As reported in the company newsletter, Heinz was aware of the potential "value-added" to its products by their association with good working conditions: "Viewed from a purely business side, these welfare features are of undoubted value. First of all their effects are to be noted in the physical and spiritual well-being of the employee. But their influence extends farther than that, engendering as it does a spirit of harmony and good will between employer and employee, the final effect of which is reflected in the Company's product, to a marked degree."[23] This "harmony" kept the Heinz family together. In advertisements, workers (both women and men) were always presented as happy at their jobs and content with their working conditions; they worked not only to gain an income for themselves but as part, according to a 1924 ad, of the "family" of Heinz, "dispensing good cheer" little different from "a hostess preparing delicious meals for favored guests." And those "hostesses" worked in the best environment. As a 1905 ad read, "Our standard process, from the field to the labeled package, is conducted along absolutely sanitary lines in model kitchens, amid surroundings that are bright and clean." Happy, white, clean, and dainty workers produced pure, clean, and good food. And in 1906, an advertisement proclaimed: "Heinz Wide-Open Kitchens ... Sunlight everywhere; spotless floors and walls; tables snowy white; shining utensils — all reflected in the excellence of Heinz 57 varieties" (see Figure 5.5).

So the corporate ethos of Heinz presented an image of the company free from the contaminants of labor unrest and dirty, unethical working conditions. Having "proper" women as its major working force, as we have seen, helped present this pure image. These women were not a threat to gender ideology; they were simply practicing their "hostess" skills for when they left the factory for their new jobs as wives. Heinz made clear that his "girls in the white cap" were preparing for their proper roles as housewives. The company offered classes for the girls in cooking and sewing, so that, "in various ways the girls are fitted for homemaking in the future."[24] Within the "family" of Heinz, in other words, women workers were daughters, in training to become proper wives. In this way, Heinz created an image of itself that set it apart from its competitors and that associated the

Cosmopolitan Magazine

HEINZ
Wide-Open Kitchens

Man has not devised a more perfectly appointed, a more cleanly and sanitary establishment than that in which Heinz Foods are prepared.

Sunlight everywhere; spotless floors and walls; tables snowy white; shining utensils—all reflected in the excellence of

From beginning to end the work of preparing the Heinz 57 Varieties is clean by system, carried out with conscientious care by the neatly-uniformed "Girl in the White Cap."

Furthermore, every Heinz Product is pure in the strictest sense of the word. They are made not only to conform to but actually exceed the requirements of all State and National Pure Food Laws.

For a real treat—and an inviting example of Heinz goodness—get from your grocer a convenient-sized crock or tin of

HEINZ
Apple Butter

Tart and piquant—not as sweet as preserves. Delicious on bread for the youngster; a luncheon appetizer for the grown-up folks. It is made of choice, selected apples; contains none but spices of our own grinding and pure granulated sugar.

Let us send you a copy of our booklet, "The Spice of Life."

H. J. HEINZ COMPANY,
New York   Pittsburgh   Chicago   London

When you write, please mention the Cosmopolitan

Figure 5.5 "Heinz, Wide-Open Kitchens," Heinz advertisement from *Cosmopolitan Magazine,* 1906. (Collection of the author)

Figure 5.6 Heinz display case in a grocery store in Yokohama, Japan, 1905. (*Pickles*, 8, 11 [1905]; Courtesy of H.J. Heinz Company)

company and the products with the highest ideals of American society: a pure, white patriarchal family that was economically stable and socially progressive.

Foreigners as Family

Heinz Company used its familial, domestic self-representation in its sales efforts overseas, and this international experience served to reinforce the image. The company simply extended its metaphor to include foreigners, making them a part of its patriarchal family, although of course a less-than-equal member. This domestic imagery took a very material form, with Heinz doing little to alter its advertising overseas, shipping, for example, life-size depictions of the Pure Heinz Vinegar girl to accompany displays of Heinz products, as is evident in figure 5.6. At the figurative level, Heinz presented its overseas sales as part of the civilizing mission, turning foreigners into members of the American family, reinforcing an image of the company's overseas expansion as part of a domesticating, civilizing ritual. By 1909, the company boasted of branch offices in London, Australia, and Hawaii and of Heinz products being carried into "the very fastnesses of darkest Africa, ... the hill camps of mining Australia and New Zealand" and "the sacred precincts of the mysterious Orient."[25] And according to the company newsletter, as Heinz products entered the homes of families in "Cuba, Puerto Rico, Mexico and Canada," they were sure to do "very effectual missionary work."[26]

The association of the selling of food products with missionary work is certainly not accidental. According to the turn-of-the-century ideology of civilization, the purchase and use of Western commodities was integral to the process of conversion — "savages" could become "civilized" through their use and display of Western products.[27] Heinz Company took full advantage of this opportunity to promote sales of its goods outside the "civilized world." At first, the primary targets were white colonists living in such settler colonies as South Africa, where "uncontaminated" foods were readily sold to consumers who had been warned in manuals and medical texts of the possible health problems associated with food grown and prepared under native conditions.[28] But Heinz also looked to the potentially much larger market of "native" populations for increased sales. As early as 1902, Heinz was expressing a "belief in an almost unlimited demand among the millions of the earth for American Food Products of superior quality — a demand possibly approaching if not equal to present home consumption."[29]

By all accounts, Henry Heinz was a firm believer in the ideology of civilization. As previously discussed, he envisioned his company as a patriarchal family, the ultimate sign of "civilization." He, of course, was the patriarch, taking care of the women and children — his workers. A speech he gave to his salesmen in 1899, titled "Development of Character," could have been written by "civilization's" avatar, Teddy Roosevelt: Heinz spoke of the "influences which tend to the upbuilding of sterling manhood, that manhood which is ready for emergencies ... without faltering" and directed his men to the "noble ideal held by self control."[30] His workers were his "children" and he provided for them — not only their social welfare but also their education, their uplifting. As mentioned earlier, Heinz offered classes for his workers in the evenings, in order to cultivate in them a taste for "culture" and prepare them, particularly the women, for their lives outside the factory. According to the company's newsletter, Heinz hung some of his art collection in the girls' dining room because he "wishes them to feel at home, and believes the effect of these surroundings will be beneficial, brightening their lives, and that they will carry into their own homes a knowledge and appreciation of the beautiful."[31]

By envisioning the company as a proper, patriarchal family, the domestic embodiment of civilization, the selling of products overseas could be presented as a benevolent, neighborly gesture. The company employed Margaret McLeod to accompany overseas Heinz's top sales representative, Alexander MacWillie. Hired as a "demonstrator," McLeod played the role of the Victorian wife (see Figure 5.7). She served food and prepared meals for "guests" in Africa, Australia, South Africa, India, Siam, and Japan, doing, in the words of the Heinz newsletter, the "missionary work of spreading the Heinz gospel of food excellence among hitherto benighted nations."[32] As a proper Victorian wife, she was first and foremost pure and white. Commenting on her visit, an editorial in the *South African News* titled "Pure Food and Pure Grit" was reprinted in the Heinz newsletter. It opens with the following: "There is a dainty young girl with golden hair in white cap and tucker who stands behind a table in J.D. Cartwright & Co.'s grocery store." She lays "a snowy cloth on the table, and silver urns and spoons." Aligning her purity with cleanliness, the essay goes on to discuss the samples of food that she is preparing and serving, adding that "the world has heard of the smoke and the dirt and the untidiness of factories, and calls out for pure food. Heinz is coming along with it!" In the same article, MacWillie fills in the author with propaganda about Heinz, where "the workers are a huge family" and where "the object of the Heinz Co. was not first to establish a world-wide trade, but, first, pure food products. The other is following."[33]

In addition to embodying the whiteness and purity of Victorian femininity, McLeod performed the role. McLeod's sales techniques, if one would call them such, literally were about "demonstrating" white, civilized domesticity — she prepared and served food to "guests" in a manner appropriate to the highest ideals of "civilized" womanhood. At times, these demonstrations took grandiose forms, transforming business transactions into soirees. In these instances, McLeod was presented as the supreme hostess. For example, the company's newsletter reported on MacWillie's and McLeod's visit to Bangkok in 1906: not long after they had begun their "usual operations" by "giving demonstrations in the Oriental stores," word spread to the king, who sent his brother and several princes to sample the food. He then issued a "royal edict commanding the Heinz representatives to serve a banquet of their famous foods in the Royal Palace." The 2-hour banquet, consisting totally of Heinz products (as the newsletter states, this was not an "ordinary demonstration, nor in any sense a conventional Siamese meal"), resulted in "the largest orders ever received for Heinz goods from a single household."[34] According to the

Figure 5.7   Photograph of Margaret McLeod, 1903. (*The 57*, 7, 4 [1903]; Courtesy of H.J. Heinz Company)

newsletter, this type of overseas experience for Heinz was not unusual, but instead was "typical of the receptions accorded Heinz representatives wherever they have gone."[35] In a letter McLeod wrote back to Heinz about the Siamese banquet, she discussed how she attended to such domestic details as menu cards, "pinning to the regular menu card a little pickle girl dressed in pink silk, the King's color, with large poke bonnet, the hand holding a tin of soup cut out, with a little white ivory elephant suspended from the fingers. White elephant is sacred to Siam and she took the fancy of the King completely."[36] As a proper hostess, she paid attention to the color and design of menu cards; as a good employee, she made to sure to include the symbols of Heinz (the pickle girl and the tin of soup). Her demonstrations of "civilization" — Heinz foods and Victorian femininity — were reinforced with visual and verbal advertisements that, as we have seen, stressed over and over the association of Heinz foods with purity, whiteness, and civilization. According to the company, the geographic spread of Heinz products was coincident with the spread of civilization: "wherever civilization exists throughout the world, in ever-broadening lines, by slow degrees and often imperceptibly, the justly termed 'World Famous 57 Varieties' have spread."[37]

Margaret McLeod was not a crass saleswoman, but the perfect embodiment of Victorian notions of womanhood, fulfilling her proper role as the civilizer of society. The impeccably dressed MacWillie, with McLeod at his side, presented a picture of the ideal couple spreading the gospel of American civilization: pure and womanly women, enterprising and manly men, engagement in the "highest" stage of economy (industrialization), and purity made visible as whiteness in distinction to those "others," both abroad and at home. In this way, Heinz presented its sales overseas as domestic, social visits. Foreigners were refashioned into neighbors, and encounters with foreign cultures were presented as friendly feasts.

Holidays with Heinz

Touring Europe on vacation — taking the "grand tour" — was not unusual for upper-class Americans in the last quarter of the 19th century, so it comes as no great surprise that the founders and presidents of American international companies had firsthand experience of overseas markets. Henry Heinz's biographer, Robert Alberts, for example, titled his chapter on Heinz's first trip overseas "Innocence Abroad, or, Mr. and Mrs. Heinz on the Grand Tour."[38] In fact, Heinz was a prolific traveler, visiting Europe every year but four between 1890 and 1914,[39] and traveling beyond the safety of Western Europe to such countries as Mexico, Egypt, Palestine, Japan, China, Korea, and Russia. Although not quite as peripatetic, George Eastman (president of Kodak) and Cyrus McCormick also traveled extensively through Europe and parts of Asia, combining their interest in international business with their leisure travel. Geographical knowledge gained from touring, as many scholars have noted,[40] is not necessarily the most reliable in terms of facts and figures, but the personal experiences of cultures beyond the United States did give these entrepreneurs something much more tangible and manifest than knowledge gained from books — a sense of how other countries functioned and an awareness of ways of life different from those in the United States. It also provided them with firsthand experience of potential business opportunities overseas.

What is most interesting in the case of Heinz is the close relationship between the representation of Henry Heinz's personal world travels and the representations of the company's international experiences. In both cases, international experiences were presented as merging business and pleasure, as traveling mixed with selling. This motif illustrates the company's attempts to represent itself as a family, with Heinz as the father, and the employees as the children, all working for the good of the whole. Overseas sales trips, using the metaphor of family, are presented as travels abroad to visit relatives. In other words, Heinz's stories about foreign cultures and countries were shaped by the company's paternal and patriarchal corporate culture.

By envisioning the company as a proper, patriarchal family, the domestic embodiment of civilization, the selling of products overseas could be presented as a benevolent, neighborly gesture. But neighbors thousands of miles apart are unable to simply "drop" by and leave food products. Heinz's overseas distribution and sales proceeded through complex channels, involving sophisticated financial exchanges and complex transportation networks. Yet, like the refashioning of its women laborers into familial sisters and mothers, Heinz Company refashioned the commercial processes through which its products were sold internationally into familial, leisurely travels.

Certainly this is how Heinz's first forays into international markets are represented in Henry Heinz's biography. According to Robert Alberts, who based much of his biography on Heinz's diaries, Henry Heinz just happened to make some international sales of his products while he was leisurely traveling overseas. With a successful food manufacturing company already established, Heinz's first trip abroad in 1886 was to Germany, home to both of his parents, who had immigrated to central Pennsylvania. He traveled with his wife and children, first to England, spending two formative weeks in London, according to Alberts.[41] Besides seeing the major sights with his family, Heinz visited by himself several food distributors and factories. He also took it upon himself to try to make a sale of his goods (apparently bringing his sales "kit" and samples with him) at Fortnum & Mason, the premier grocer in London. He apparently was surprised when he was successful at selling them all seven products, including horseradish, ketchup, and chili sauce.[42] This was Heinz's first overseas sales and, in Alberts' biography, it is presented as just a little "visit" that happened to have occurred while Heinz was in London. In Germany, Heinz combined sightseeing and family visits with trips to food plants, farms, retail stores and, interestingly, a Singer Sewing Machine factory in Durlach.[43] He took detailed notes in his diary about farming methods, wage structure for various occupations, and transportation improvements. He also conducted business, arranging for a German food company to distribute Heinz products in Germany. Leaving his family members in Germany, he visited several cities in the Netherlands, including Amsterdam, where, after seeing cauliflower unloaded on the docks, he visited the farms where they were cultivated and arranged for 200 casks of them to be shipped to Pittsburgh.[44] He then traveled to Heidelberg, collected his family, and returned via Brussels, Antwerp, London, and Liverpool, where they boarded their ship for home. Heinz's first overseas business deals, then, were all performed personally — Heinz's sale at Fortnum & Mason, his arrangement of a distribution house in Germany, and the importing of cauliflower from the Netherlands. These were certainly small beginnings, and Heinz Company did not become international in any significant way until the late 1890s, but the strong appeal of seeing how business was done outside the United States, and of analyzing potential markets up close and personal, became characteristics of the company's "culture" of internationalism. The representation of these business deals — as if they just happened while on tour — also became part of the company's corporate culture.

Heinz's second major trip outside the United States in 1893 was explicitly for business purposes. He was part of a group of 50 businessmen invited to tour Mexico with the aim of fostering American investment. Most of what they toured were businesses operated by European capital. Heinz concluded that Mexico was not a market to be pursued, given its high duty on imports: "Mexico offers a very poor field for my goods. To be profitable and to pay for working up, I should have the trade of the masses, but the duty on all our goods is so heavy that they become expensive luxuries, and are used as such here. Pickles that retail in the States at 25 cents per bottle must sell at 90 cents here. Catsup that retails 25 cents there is sold here at $1."[45] Periodically, throughout the next 15 years or so, Henry Heinz traveled to Europe and Asia with his family for leisure trips, though the trips were often punctuated by business concerns and by what he would call "missionary work." Heinz was a devout man, interested in participating in the missionary work of spreading Christianity, and with it civilization, around the world. So when he traveled abroad, Heinz was always assessing the need for, or the successes of, Christian schools and missions, in addition to potential new commercial outlets. In fact, he believed that the spread of his business both indicated and helped to bring about the diffusion of a Christian and civilized world. For example, during his most extensive trip in 1913, Heinz spent 6 months traveling through Japan, China, Russia, Poland, and Germany, ending in Switzerland so he could attend the World Sunday School Association (WSSA) convention. Heinz had long been a member and supporter of this international association (most of its 28 million members were drawn from the United States and Europe), whose main goal was to establish Christian Sunday schools throughout the world. The trip itself was planned partly so that Heinz and several fellow members of the WSSA could visit some of the schools they had established in Asia. For Henry Heinz, therefore, international travel was as much about business and religion as it was about touring. He saw no contradiction between these three aspects of his life. This merging of commerce, religion, and travel both reflected and reinforced Heinz Company's self-representation as a proper, hence Christian, patriarchal family, whose overseas sales were as much missionary work as they were commercial ventures. This becomes more evident in a survey of the company's newsletter.

Many of the pages that filled the Heinz Company's in-house newsletter (called *Pickles* when it was first issued in 1897, then changed to *The 57* in 1903, and later called *The 57 Life*) were dedicated to documenting Heinz's increasing foreign business, but these documentations were invariably presented as travel stories, narrated not necessarily by Heinz himself but by his sons or his employees. Between 1901 and 1903, for example, five different travel accounts were printed in the newsletter. The first story appeared in June 1901, in an article entitled "Heinz in South Africa." The two-page story reported on the travels of Stanley Monteith, who had "traveled for us a number of years in America and England, as well as in South Africa."[46] The article is prefaced with a photograph of Monteith in a white linen suit and hat, sitting in a wheeled cart, being pulled by a "native" (see Figure 5.8). The photo, which has a caption reading, "Showing how our representative in South Africa travel," is a posed shot, resembling a snapshot taken of tourists, not businessmen. The article, though, is hardly about those "travels" per se, but instead starts by documenting where Heinz is based in South Africa, how shipments are made into the interior ("the goods are carried by steamer to the mouth of the Zambesi, boated up the river, and then packed by mules or natives overland"[47]), the appreciative customers of these goods, and the success of the sales. The second half of the article reads like a geography lesson, with discussions of the climate, soils, and agriculture of the Cape Colony: "It may interest our readers to learn of the general character and climate of Cape Colony. It is dry, highly salubrious and milder than in England; the atmosphere is clear and buoyant."[48] It ends with a short paragraph that expresses sentiments found throughout the newsletter: "Our 359 travelers are scat-

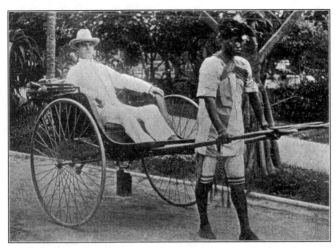

Figure 5.8 Photograph of Stanley Monteith in South Africa, 1901. (*Pickles*, 5, 4 [1901]; Courtesy of H.J. Heinz Company)

tered over the civilized world from Alaska to the Cape of Good Hope, supplying Pure Food, 57 different kinds, prepared by Heinz."[49]

The second travel story was a report from Heinz's sons, who had just returned from a trip to Japan and China. Howard Heinz had apparently given a talk about his travels to the employees of the company, and the newsletter reported on the highlights of this presentation:

> Dwelling briefly upon his travels, he spoke of the different countries, the characteristics of the people, the financial and religious aspects of the present day, and of the wonderful strides that Japan is making in its endeavor to become a factor among the civilized powers; and is hoping for the day to come when its sister country, China, shall awaken from the lethargy that has prevailed among its people for thousands of years and shall come to the front as a civilized, religious and financial power among the nations.[50]

In October of the same year (1902), a third story appeared, this time featuring the travels of Alexander MacWillie in Japan. The newsletter had previously mentioned that MacWillie, who had just returned from the West Indies, would be sailing from San Francisco to "carry the '57 varieties' around the world,"[51] visiting Hawaii, China, Japan, India, and Australia, a trip that was anticipated to take two years. The two-page article mirrored the first report about Monteith, most strikingly by the opening photograph in which MacWillie poses in the exact manner of Monteith (see Figure 5.9) — in a full suit,

Figure 5.9   Photograph of Alexander MacWillie in Japan, 1902. (*Pickles*, 6, 6 [1902]; Courtesy of H.J. Heinz Company)

sitting in a rickshaw, being pulled by a "native,"[52] suggesting the leisurely nature of MacWillie's visit. Entitled "Foreign Trade in American Products," the article first summarized the state of the American export trade in general, before moving to Heinz's history of overseas sales — how the company started with nearby markets, such as Canada, then moved to South America and onto more distant markets, making direct reference to Monteith's previous journey: "Later on, we extended operations by various means to South Africa, India, the Straits Settlements, and in some degree to the countries, still further east, personally visiting the South African colonies nearly two years ago through a special representative this being at the time the longest single trip ever undertaken by a Heinz traveler."[53] Notice again the reference of Heinz's sales force as travelers who make personal visits. This manner of representing sales trips as leisurely voyages continues. MacWillie's travels are referred to as an "'around the world' trip,"[54] whereas other salespeople are called "'globe trotters.'"[55] The merging of business with pleasure through travel is evident in the article's final paragraph (the opening quote from this chapter):

> Through samples, carried sometimes by our own representatives and at others by "globe trotters" from the great commission houses of London and New York; sometimes by missionaries or tourists, and frequently by means we are unable to trace, our products have found their way, literally to the

ends of the earth, and we claim with justifiable pride that the name of "Heinz" has become known in every country and to every nation of the world.[56]

That slippage between "globe trotter" and company representative is even more apparent in an article titled "Around the World with Heinz Pickle Charms" that appeared in March of 1902. This piece differed from the others in that it was written in the first-person, authored by Harry Steele Morrison (a popular writer), and was illustrated not with photos but with sketches of scenes on his trip. The story follows Morrison's travels on board a ship that docks at several locations, including Spain, Morocco, Malta, Aden (Yemen), and Colombo (Sri Lanka), and the action of the story involves Morrison giving away pickle charms as payment, diversion, or tips to the "natives" at each place. It is only clear at the end of the story that Morrison is a working as a Heinz representative: "I have never bestowed one which was unappreciated, and hereafter when any of my Heinz friends travel abroad, I advise them to carry a supply of Heinz pickle charms. They are charms in fact as well as name, and make easy the path of the traveler."[57] No Heinz "facts" are presented in this article, although the author provided descriptions of each place and its inhabitants, similar to many such travel stories that appeared in contemporary illustrated magazines, such as *Harper's Weekly* or *Munsey's Magazine*.

A fifth story that appeared in 1903 returned to the style of the first ones, opening with a photograph of MacWillie in a open-air carriage, dressed again in a white linen suit, although this time in a wagon pulled by a horse; a "native" boy is shown sitting in the back seat (see Figure 5.10). The very brief narrative that accompanied the photo tells of the recent travels of MacWillie in Australia and his success in introducing Heinz to the country through the use of "demonstrations" — free samples of Heinz products given away in grocer's stores and at lunch counters. The person who actually accomplished these "demonstrations" was, as noted previously, Margaret McLeod. As a middle-class white American woman, McLeod was presented in Heinz's newsletter as the embodiment of purity and goodness, a fitting symbol for Heinz products, and the travels of MacWillie and McLeod were written about as if they were family visits, not sales trips. This further solidified the image of Heinz's overseas business dealings as simply extensions of leisurely travel.

A similar series of travel reports in 1906 and 1907 featured stories of MacWillie and McLeod in East Asia. Continuing the motif of the native/rickshaw touristic portrait, a December 1906 article

Figure 5.10   Photograph of Alexander MacWillie in Australia, 1903. (*The 57*, 7, 3 [1903];
Courtesy of H.J Heinz Company)

opens with a photo of McLeod dressed in a proper suit and hat being
pulled in a rickshaw by a "native" (see Figure 5.11). This image is
particularly interesting because it is a direct imitation of a Kodak
advertisement from 1905 (see Figure 5.12). McLeod is presented as
the Kodak girl, *the* advertising icon that Kodak used during this time
period (and up until the second half of the 20th century) to help "fem-
inize" its product — that is, to show that its cameras were so simple to
operate that even middle-class women could become proficient pho-
tographers. As Nancy West has argued, the Kodak girl was part New
Woman — an independent, outdoorsy, athletic woman — and part
traditional woman — a well-dressed, attractive, decorative woman.[58]
This served to make her an ideal symbol for Kodak, softening the
company's technological image, while associating it with progress
— arguably the same role that McLeod, and, as we have seen, the
"pure" Heinz girl, served for Heinz Company. The contrast of the
white, well-dressed woman with the non-white man, and her positioning atop the rickshaw, certainly points to the woman's superiority, reinforcing traditional views of Japanese culture as lower in

Figure 5.11   Photograph of Margaret McLeod in Siam, 1906. (*The 57 Life*, 2, 4 [1906]; Courtesy of H.J. Heinz Company)

the civilizational hierarchy. Yet, as West points out, the two figures are presented as quite similar to each other: "The similarity of their expressions, poses, and even facial features forms a stunning focal point for this advertisement, suggesting as it does the confluence of American and Japanese beauty."[59] So the Kodak girl is touring a country of great interest to Americans because it is exotic and yet somehow also similar, on the verge of westernization. Depicting McLeod in the identical position (though interestingly this image shows McLeod in Siam, not Japan) reinforces Heinz Company's representation of its overseas business practices as consisting of "travelers" touring exotic yet about to be familiar places, with both workers and potential consumers part of the "family" of Heinz.

The article that accompanies this image takes the form of a letter home, reaffirming this familial quality. McLeod's letter begins,

Figure 5.12   "The Kodak Girl in Fair Japan," Kodak advertisement, 1905. (Business Information Center, Eastman Kodak Company)

"Since our arrival in Bangkok, Sept. 21, we have been in one continuous whirl." She goes on to discuss their "whirl" of activities as if they were all social occasions, including a banquet for the king and his family, where Heinz products were served. But, of course, mixed in with these social reports were two other types of information — one pertaining to the increasing success of Heinz in penetrating foreign markets and the other relating geographical information about those markets. Oftentimes, these two types of information merged into what could be called a "commercial geography." McLeod ends her letter "home" with an assessment of the future marketability of Heinz products in Siam, comparing it favorably to that of India: "We ... entertain great expectations for future business in Siam. It is one of the Eastern countries where we hope to get business from the natives. They have no caste prejudices and take to European customs with favor. Once we get them started, they will consume more of the '57 Varieties' than all India."[60] McLeod combines her discussion of cultural customs with business assessments, a motif common in these newsletter reports and also, as we have seen, in the worldviews of other early international corporations.

This merging of geographical information and economic forecasts — this commercial geography — is most apparent in MacWillie's three-part series of travel narratives written for the newsletter in 1906. In these rather lengthy (relative to other pieces in the newsletter) accounts of his visits to Hong Kong, Manila, Singapore, Batavia, Japan, China, and India, MacWillie described general living conditions, cultural customs, transportation routes, architectural sites, and historical trajectories, before offering his view of each country's economic outlook. After describing the "old" Japan from his first visit there in 1901 ("only in childhood," MacWillie wrote, "when Fairyland was still a place of easy exploration for our tender fancies, could we have imagined a country so full of amazing charms and unceasing delights as that which spreads itself out before the traveler on his first visit"[61]), MacWillie turned his attention to the new business acumen apparent in the culture of Japan of 1905, the year that Japan defeated Russia, marking the country's westernization: "Business men talked of the prices of stocks and bonds, and pluckily asserted that their industrial enterprises were preparing for commercial conquests of no less importance than their naval and military achievements had been."[62] His analysis of this new situation in Japan, caused partly, he believed, by the opening of Japanese ports to foreign commerce that had occurred in the past 60 years, led him to offer these final thoughts:

Japan of the Nineteenth Century is rapidly passing away, and Japan of the Twentieth Century is developing to an extent not even surpassed by the growth of our own great republic. Ten years ago the total export and import trade of Japan amounted to 70 million dollars; in 1906 the total exports and imports amounted to 420 million dollars, of which, by the way, America secured over 97 million or nearly one fourth of Japan's entire over-sea trade.[63]

This assessment of Japan's changing economic climate — one that is favorably compared even to the United States — reveals MacWillie's interest in the business potential of the country for Heinz trade, an assessment that parallels Henry Heinz's own views of the country that were apparent from his travels there. But MacWillie saw the potential for favorable business climates in almost all the places he visited, even though he was not loathe to point out the cultural or social problems that might get in the way.

MacWillie opened his China narrative by relating his initial reactions from his ship, reactions that revealed a range of racist stereotypes: "Nearing the shore we see huge, ungainly looking junks with tattered sails go lumbering by, their dirty pig-tailed crews lounging over the rails from piles of straw matting and highly odoriferous heaps of dried fish. Along the banks are villages of mud huts emitting fearful smells, with dirty water buffaloes wallowing in the mud around them."[64] Yet it only took a few paragraphs for MacWillie to move on to an assessment of the potential of the Chinese market for American producers. And, similar to the analysis of Japan, MacWillie offered this assessment of the future by comparing China today with its recent past:

The population of China is over 400 million, and the foreign trade of this enormous country is rapidly increasing. From a total of 150 million dollars in 1896 the exports and imports increased to over 500 million dollars in 1906, of which the United States secured in the latter years about one seventh of the entire foreign trade. Railways, which play such an important part in the development of any country, are being projected in all directions throughout China, and the shriek of the locomotive whistle is to-day heard in places where only ten years ago an European was hardly heard of and never seen. If you are curious to see the China of opium smokers, dried rats, and women of small feet, you must make haste, for such things will be among the vanished customs and curiosities of the country twenty years hence.[65]

Here MacWillie gave voice to the discourse of progress, of what he assumed was the inevitable movement through time and space, measured by technology and trade, toward a modern future for China. The past would vanish with the help of the West in favor of the future, where "the shriek of the locomotive whistle" would be heard everywhere.

This became more clear when MacWillie visited the Philippines, where he emphasized the positive changes that occurred in Manila since the American "invasion," including the education of children ("the number of children attending public schools has increased in the same time from forty thousand to over three hundred thousand"[66]), railway development, and of course the fact that "exports from the United States to the Philippines have increased in ten years from one million dollars to twenty million dollars."[67] Of Java, and its capital Batavia (Jakarta), MacWillie wrote, "The Dutch have brought with them from their native country that uncompromising aversion to dirt that characterizes them as a race, and Batavia in this respect is simply a bit of the mother country transplanted in another clime."[68] Similarly, in MacWillie's last "Oriental sketch," he described his travels in India and recited a history of a passionate country that needed the supervision of Great Britain: "Its history is a tangled tale of force, fraud, cunning, desperate love and more desperate revenge, crimes worthy of demons and virtues fit for gods, which only the control of the British Empire within the past hundred years has been able to direct into saner and more temperate ways."[69] According to MacWillie, the "saner" ways of Great Britain included the development of a well-equipped and spatially diffuse railroad network that linked all parts of the country. This was particularly valuable for businesses, like Heinz, whose products could be shipped relatively easily from one part of India to another. MacWillie made sure to include a small discussion of the success of Heinz sales in relation to the new railroads, mentioning that Heinz products were for sale in 75 of the railroad station restaurants and were served in the dining cars. The best palates, both Indian and British, were growing accustomed to the "high standard of quality"[70] of Heinz products: "Maharajahs, Nizams, native Princes and English army officers everywhere throughout the empire are extensive users of Heinz products."[71]

The range of travel stories that were printed in Heinz's newsletter gives some evidence of how the company envisioned the geography of foreign markets, and its own place within those markets. Heinz's emissaries overseas were simply touring different countries, observing local customs, visiting the sites, and meeting the "natives." With the Heinz Corporation depicted as a patriarchal family, its factory as a large home, and its sales representatives as hosts and hostesses, the entry of Heinz products into foreign countries was not so much an economic invasion as it was a neighborly, social visit. The discourse of civilization that positioned different cultures in a "natural" hierarchy provided the necessary linguistic tools and organizational framework for these travel tales. Such countries as India, the Philippines, and China were on their way to reaching civilization with the direct "help" of colonial, Western powers, while places such as Japan were developing with the indirect influence of Western culture.

Yet within all these discussions, civilization is measured as much by economic growth as by markers of race, culture, or religion. These examples show how the discourse of civilization was wrapped up in analyses of economics and commerce. Heinz himself, in his travels, mixed business with his missionary work, and MacWillie wrote about the economic growth potential of such countries as China and Japan. The geographical knowledge of the world produced through Heinz's newsletter, in other words, sorted out the nations into a hierarchy based on economic development, where all nations theoretically were on the way to reaching civilization. Because of Heinz's particular corporate culture that had been developed to help sell manufactured food (the company as a domestic family), that geographical knowledge took the form of travel narratives. In this way, foreign nations are figured as tourist sites, exotic yet unthreatening. The image that accompanied a 1908 ad for Mandalay sauce (see Figure 5.13), for example, encapsulated a touristic view of the Far East, including palm trees, elephants, and temples. Unlike Singer and McCormick, Heinz never produced advertisements that showed foreigners using their products and thereby becoming "modern," yet it also did not present images of foreigners as "primitive." Even though it was clear from the company's newsletter that Heinz's executives were aware of and interested in the modernizing and "civilizing" processes at work in many countries, they chose not to depict that in their advertisements. Instead, they depicted foreign lands as fun travel destinations. Heinz Company found the association with the foreign useful as a way of tempting American women to "tour" the world through their consumption of exotic foods.

Heinz boasted in a 1924 advertisement that its products could now be found in "every civilized country in the world." In fact, as we have seen, the very presence of Heinz products in a particular country connoted its status as "civilized," or at least civilizable. Heinz's internationalism reinforced the ideology of civilization/savagery that

From Far=Off Mandalay

Nothing quite so piquant and appetizing ever surprised the palate as a touch of Heinz Mandalay Sauce—the new table luxury whose rare Oriental savor has made it the popular condiment of the day.

HEINZ
Mandalay Sauce

is composed of choicest fruits, vegetables and spices of foreign and domestic origin, skilfully blended after a recipe found by an English army officer in the Far East.

It imparts incomparable goodness to hot or cold meats, fish, game, soups and gravies. Indispensable for all chafing-dish cooking—Welsh rarebits, cheese toast, and so on. Stimulates the jaded appetite; is unquestionably wholesome.

Try a bottle from your grocer; it is far removed from common sauces—unlike any other in flavor.

HEINZ

57

Are put up without coloring matter or preservatives.

Other seasonable Heinz delicacies are Sweet Pickles, Preserved Fruits, Jellies, Cranberry Sauce, Euchred Figs, Tomato Chutney, etc. Our free booklet, "The Spice of Life," tells all about them.

H. J. HEINZ COMPANY,

New York   Pittsburgh   Chicago   London

Figure 5.13   "From Far-Off Mandalay," Heinz advertisement from *The Review of Reviews*, 1908. (Collection of the author)

placed the cultures of the world in an evolutionary hierarchy (cultures that adopted the "benefits" of industrial production, such as "pure" food, were on their way to becoming civilized) and, in turn, that ideology legitimized the company's internationalism (spreading the "benefits" of white, Anglo culture was part of the civilizing mission). H.J. Heinz Company was certainly not alone in using this ideology to promote its products at home and overseas. Indeed, it was endemic to the process of American informal imperialism. Yet because this was a processed food company, Heinz developed particular promotional strategies. To decrease anxieties over contamination, Heinz opened its plant to public scrutiny. To decrease anxieties over making visible women laborers, it presented them as little different from their consuming sisters. In these ways, Heinz Company was successful in presenting itself as the embodiment of a civilized company, carrying on the civilizing mission of spreading the "benefits" of Western society by sending its products out to explore the world, and of course, in the meantime, to create new markets. It also produced an image of foreign nations and cultures as tourist sites, both familiar and exotic at the same time, different from yet on their way to becoming similar to the cultures of the United States. Heinz represented its corporate "family" therefore as ever-expandable, reaching out to the "fastnesses of darkest Africa" and the "sacred precincts of the mysterious Orient"[72] to convert savages into civilized people. In turn, this "missionary work"[73] served to reinforce the company's patriarchal and paternal corporate culture.

Endnotes

1. Harvey A. Levenstein, *A Revolution at the Table: The Transformation of the American Diet* (New York: Oxford University Press, 1988).
2. Ibid., 39.
3. Robert C. Alberts, *The Good Provider: H.J. Heinz and His 57 Varieties* (Boston: Houghton Mifflin, 1973), 79.
4. Levenstein (1988).
5. Alberts (1973), 149.
6. Levenstein (1988).
7. Ibid., 35.
8. Ibid., 35.
9. Alberts (1973).
10. David Goodman and Michael Redclift, *Refashioning Nature: Food, Ecology, and Culture* (New York: Routledge, 1991).
11. See, for example, Susanne Freidberg, "Cleaning Up Down South: Supermarkets, Ethical Trade and African Horticulture," *Social and Cultural Geography*, 4, 1 (2003): 27–44.

12. "All Records for Visitors Broken," *The 57*, 10, 3 (1906).
13. "Girl's Dining Hall," *Pickles*, 1, 9 (October, 1897).
14. Ibid.
15. *Pickles*, 1, 7 (July, 1897).
16. Ibid.
17. Of course, Heinz Company was not alone in promoting a form of corporate paternalism. In the United States, similar practices and discourses can be traced to the early textile factories in Lowell and Waltham established by the Boston Associates in the 1820s, and in Britain such "enlightened" practices could be found in such places as Lever's Port Sunlight. It does seem that the working conditions at Heinz may have been better than at other manufacturing plants. In a 1909 study of working conditions for women in Pittsburgh, the Heinz plant was described in a relatively positive manner, almost echoing the company's promotional rhetoric: "The walls of light brick, scrupulously cleaned, stand out against the murky background of the city; and within doors, the light walls, wide windows, and spotless white of work tables bear out first impressions that the management has high standards both for the surroundings of its work-people and the quality of it product." (See E.B. Butler, *Women and the Trades: Pittsburgh, 1907-08* [New York: The Russell Sage Foundation, 1909]). The point is that the practices of corporate paternalism were integral to the promotion of Heinz as a "good" and "clean" place to manufacture "good" and "clean" food.
18. Mary Poovey, *Uneven Developments: The Ideological Work of Gender in Mid-Victorian England* (Chicago: University of Chicago Press, 1988).
19. Sidney Mintz, *Sweetness and Power: The Place of Sugar in Modern History* (New York: Viking Press, 1985).
20. Anne McClintock, *Imperial Leather: Race, Gender, and Sexuality in the Colonial Contest* (New York: Routledge, 1995).
21. Ibid., 211.
22. "The Auditorium," *Pickles*, 4, 5 (January, 1900).
23. "The Spirit of the 57," *The 57*, 40th anniversary number (1909).
24. Ibid.
25. "The 57 Varieties across Seas," *The 57*, 40th anniversary number (1909).
26. *Pickles*, 3, 7 (August, 1899).
27. For an elaboration of this idea, see Matthew Frye Jacobson, *Barbarian Virtues: The United States Encounters Foreign Peoples at Home and Abroad, 1876–1917* (New York: Hill and Wang, 2000) and Timothy Burke, *Lifebuoy Men, Lux Women: Commodification, Consumption, and Cleanliness in Modern Zimbabwe* (Durham, NC: Duke University Press, 1996).
28. Susanne Freidberg, "French Beans for the Masses: A Modern Historical Geography of Food in Burkina Faso," *Journal of Historical Geography*, 29, 3 (2003): 445–463.

29. "Foreign Trade in American Products," *Pickles*, 6, 6 (October, 1902).
30. "New York Weekly Convention," *Pickles*, 3, 2 (December, 1899).
31. *Pickles*, 3, 4 (June, 1899).
32. "What the 57 Are Doing in Foreign Countries," *The 57 Life*, 2, 4 (December, 1906).
33. "The '57 in South Africa," *The 57*, 7, 4 (September, 1903).
34. "Abroad with the 57," *The 57*, 10, 3 (1906).
35. Ibid.
36. "What the 57 Are Doing in Foreign Countries," *The 57 Life*, 2, 4 (December, 1906).
37. "Foreign Trade in American Products," *Pickles*, 6, 6 (October, 1902).
38. Alberts (1973).
39. Ibid., 105.
40. See, for example, Felix Driver's *Geography Militant: Cultures of Exploration and Empire* (Malden, MA: Blackwell, 2001) and David N. Livingstone's *The Geographical Tradition: Episodes in the History of a Contested Empire* (Cambridge, MA: Blackwell, 1993).
41. As Alberts (1973, 76), writes, "For this city Henry Heinz developed an affection that was to bring him back year after year for three decades to come."
42. Ibid., 79.
43. Ibid., 81.
44. Ibid.
45. Quoted in Alberts (1973), 106.
46. *Pickles*, 5, 4 (June 1901): 1–2.
47. Ibid., 1–2.
48. Ibid., 2.
49. Ibid.
50. *Pickles*, 6, 2 (July 1902).
51. *Pickles*, 5, 10 (February 1902).
52. Interestingly, this photo appears to be have been taken in a photo studio, with a staged backdrop.
53. *Pickles*, 6, 6 (October, 1902): 2.
54. Ibid.
55. Ibid.
56. Ibid.
57. Harry Steele Morrison, "Around the World with Heinz Pickle Charms," *Pickles*, 5, 2 (March 1902): 3.
58. Nancy Martha West, *Kodak and the Lens of Nostalgia* (Charlottesville: University Press of Virginia, 2000).
59. Ibid., 132.
60. "What the 57 Are Doing in Foreign Countries," *The 57 Life*, 2, 4 (December 1906): 3.
61. Alexander MacWillie, "Impressions of the Orient," *The 57 Life*, 3, 2 (May, 1907): 1.

62. Ibid., 2.
63. Ibid., 4.
64. Ibid., 4.
65. Ibid., 4–5
66. Alexander MacWillie, "Hong Kong, Manila, Singapore and Batavia," *The 57 Life,* 3, 3 (June 1907): 6.
67. Ibid.
68. Ibid., 8.
69. Alexander MacWillie, "Through the Indian Empire," *The 57 Life,* 3, 4 (July 1907): 1.
70. Ibid., 3.
71. Ibid.
72. "The 57 Varieties across Seas," *The 57,* 40th anniversary number (1909).
73. *Pickles,* 3, 7 (August, 1899).

6

Flexible Racism

Commercial geography undermined the world of racial and natural exoticism by describing a more immediate international community where — despite differences — all humans and nations contributed to trade through the conquest of the land. Correspondingly, civilization began to be judged increasingly by reference to commerce.
— Susan Schulten, *The Geographical Imagination in America, 1880–1950* (Chicago: University of Chicago Press, 2001), 12.

With the whole of mankind now included in the "development" paradigm, legitimacy was "naturalized" and rooted in a universality much less open to question than the political intrigues of a so-called international organization.
— Gilbert Rist, *The History of Development from Western Origins to Global Faith* (London: Zed Books, 1999), 75.

In the first decades of the 20th century, geography textbooks in America shifted their emphasis from racial categorizations of countries to economic ones, with the nations of the world "organized around commercial potential rather than racial difference."[1] As Susan Schulten argues, this new "commercial geography" both reflected and shaped the political and historical imperatives of the time. It gave intellectual legitimacy to American economic interventions overseas, while at the same time being fashioned through this new internationalism.[2] By making natural a worldview of potential "sameness" through commerce, this new commercial geography was constitutive of America's emerging economic empire.

As I have argued throughout this book, a similar reimagining of the world was evident in other texts and in other times. From the

1880s onward, many American international companies presented foreigners as potential customers and foreign cultures as potentially modern. Hardly the stuff of geography textbooks or the pages of *National Geographic*, corporate advertisements, catalogs, and trade cards were nonetheless filled with information about the commercial potential of the world. This geographical information was not abstracted into maps to form atlases, nor was it organized by the systematic categories of world regional geographies, nor did it attempt to disguise its commercial intent. Instead, this geographical knowledge took the more direct and personal form of telling stories about people who could become "white" through consumption, a sort of "flexible racism." Confined neither to schools nor the pages of "intellectual" magazines, these stories circulated globally through the same networks of commerce that they legitimized.

Although clearly connected to the larger politics of American foreign policy, as Schulten suggests of the new commercial, "scientific geography" lessons, these stories functioned also at the everyday level of "politics," circulating through the homes and apartments of working and middle-class Americans throughout the country. Depicting foreigners as consumers made them familiar, potentially part of the "universal" family of modernity. And these stories of familiarity through consumption were long lived. As Gilbert Rist[3] suggests, this universality based on commerce served as a key component of the discourses that legitimized economic development policies of the United States after World War II. In this concluding chapter, I draw out the "lessons" that this flexible view of the world taught Americans and show how these popular, commodity-driven stories were critical to the iterative process that made natural America's imperial commercial ambitions.

When middle-class woman like Hattie Avard from Verona, New York (see Figure 4.33 and 4.34), and Mrs. Helen A. Chase of Haverhill, Massachusetts (see Figure 1.1), looked through the advertisements printed in their weekly magazines and circulating throughout their homes, they no doubt were participating in and reinforcing what Anne McClintock has called "commodity racism" — that is, the presentation of the "narrative of imperial Progress" converted into "consumer spectacle."[4] It was a process that turned the middle-class home into a "space of the display of imperialism and the reinvention of race."[5] Much of this reinvention was accomplished through advertisements of commodities that gained meaning through their association to empire, advertisements that littered the pages of popular magazines, that were printed on trade cards and collected in scrapbooks (see Figure 6.1 to 6.3), and that decorated the goods themselves as

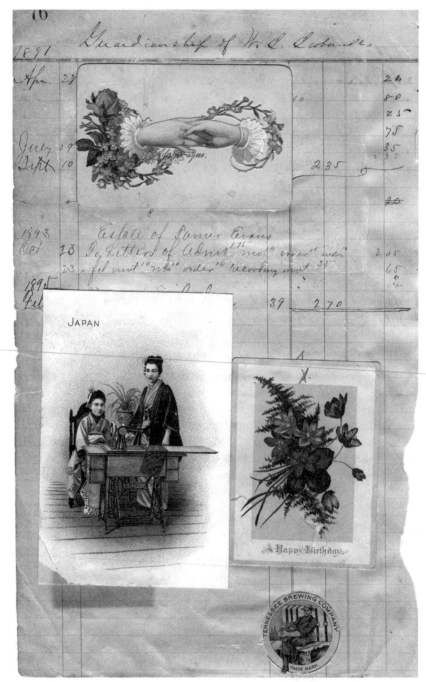

Figure 6.1 Page from a turn-of-the-century American scrapbook. (Collection of the author)

Figure 6.2   Page from a turn-of-the-century American scrapbook. (Collection of the author)

labels and signs. But so too these women were participating in what historian Kristin Hoganson has called "cosmopolitan domesticity"[6] — a powerful aesthetic movement that spoke to the desire on the part of middle- and upper-class women to express status by importing European, high-style objects into the home *and* displaying products from "exotic" regions, such as carpets from Turkey, curios from Mexico, Egyptian columns, or, for those who could not afford the objects themselves, advertisements and trade cards that depicted foreign peoples and lands. In Hoganson's words, this "cosmopolitanism implied an appreciation of other peoples' … artistic production and cultural attainments, a valorization of ethnographic and other geographic knowledge, and varying degrees of identification with people outside the United States."[7]

Both this notion of a cosmopolitanism of the home and the idea of commodity racism are based on the proliferation of commodities and advertisements made possible by imperial expansion and given meaning through that expansion, but they describe different phenomena — McClintock uses the term "commodity racism" to refer to discourses that surrounded goods whose meanings were gained through an assertion of fixed racial and cultural difference, whereas Hoganson's "cosmopolitan domesticity" refers to an aesthetic that derived its meanings through erasures of or fluidity within some of those differences. Both, it seems, were operating in American homes in the late 19th century, and both can tell us about the imbrication of race, empire, gender, commodities, and subjectivities. What I have suggested throughout this book, however, is that neither commodity racism nor cosmopolitan domesticity provide an adequate framework for describing and understanding the representations of an emerging American commercial empire that infiltrated the homes of middle- and working-class Americans and that were constitutive of their identities as white Americans. I propose a slightly different framework for understanding the representations of foreign bodies in American advertising, one based on a more malleable form of racism — a framework that I call "flexible racism." This malleable form of racism was apparent throughout the various stories I have traced in this book, and I think it provides a critical insight into what these early international companies were telling Americans about the rest of the world. In this chapter, then, I use this term "flexible racism" to draw together and interrogate the set of meanings and ideologies about the foreign that were carried by commodities and their advertisements and that were circulating in turn-of-the-century America.

The ads and commodities that women like Hattie Avard and Helen Chase viewed in their parlors relayed complicated messages about "other" peoples. Some (Native and African Americans) were for the most part completely outside the shared community, whereas others, potential participants in the commonalities of consumption, were presented as malleable subjects. Representations of these people reflected not necessarily the scientific racism of fixed difference then, but rather a more ecumenical and malleable vision — a flexible racism. But where did this vision come from? Let me briefly summarize some of the very practical ways that American companies represented the world.

All five of the international companies that I've examined shared a very practical view of global commerce, in the sense that their interests were governed almost exclusively by commercial prospects. Singer Manufacturing Company, for example, constantly reassessed and adapted its sales techniques and styles to the particular needs of certain cultures, conforming, as they said, to "hindoo" customs, and in China, to "oriental" ways of sewing clothing, whereas Cyrus McCormick and his sons personally traveled the world assessing the wheat-growing potential of regions and how McCormick machinery could be shipped to what they considered remote areas. No doubt firm adherents to the racist ideologies of the time, the owners, managers, and agents of these companies saw no contradictions between their racist, hierarchical views of the world and their assessments of potential sales. In fact, this hierarchical view of the world legitimized

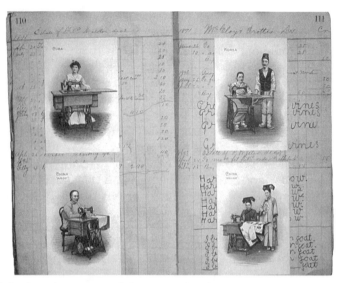

Figure 6.3   Page from a turn-of-the-century American scrapbook. (Collection of the author)

commercial expansion in the sense that they believed their products would be spreading "civilization," bringing prosperity.

The view from the late 19th century boardroom, then, was of a world inhabited by peoples sorted out by stages, yet all on the path toward "civilization," and all therefore potential consumers. In this way, their worldview united a belief in Christian millennialism (the belief that human history has one cosmic purpose, which is the millennial fight against evil), with Darwinian evolution (instead of God working toward that perfection, evolution could do the job),[8] and economic development (evolution could be helped along through, and measured by, economic stages).[9] By aligning consumption with civilization, businessmen could consider the geographic spread of their products as missionary work, and their resultant empires forged together not by conquest but by trade. This peaceful conquest was seen, in turn, as a sign that the United States itself was more civilized than its European rivals. Hence, American companies presented a racialized hierarchy that was not fixed.

This assertion of malleable identities, and therefore of changing categorizations of difference, was neither new to the late 19th century nor particular to the United States. As Roxanne Wheeler[10] argues, visible difference became a dominant way of organizing the world's peoples only in the late 18th century, before which other types of classifications (social organization, religion, clothing) coexisted with race as categories of difference. Wheeler stresses that in 18th century

Britain, categories of difference included those that afforded people a "mutability of identity" and often allowed for an "elasticity" of race.[11] She also argues for an "awareness of multiplicity,"[12] given that, in most historical situations, several ways of understanding difference often coexisted. Even within 19th century British thought, therefore, less-fixed ideas of difference must have coexisted alongside the increasingly dominant notion of fixed racial identity. What is of interest here is the consistency and dominance of these less-fixed ideas of race and difference — this flexible racism — within the discourses of American late 19th and early 20th century corporate advertising.

For example, (as discussed in Chapter 4) McCormick Harvesting Machine Company explained the differences between the United States, on the one hand, and India and China, on the other: "The commerce of progressive nations has multiplied in proportion to their use of reaping machinery. The unprogressive nations are those that have no machinery to gather their food products. China, India, and other rice-eating nations have remained stagnant during the marvelous progress of the white races, not because their people eat rice, but because their methods of producing it are so slow and laborious that all their energies are absorbed in obtaining food."[13] In other words, countries such as India and China were lower in the hierarchy not because of culture or race but because of technology, something that American companies could sell to them in the form of a commodity. This is what I am calling "flexible racism."

We can see this form of racism at work in the types of commercial assessments these companies required in order to conduct business outside the United States. In corporate boardrooms, decisions about how and where to export products required very practical physical and cultural geographical knowledge. H.J. Heinz Company, for example, sent out emissaries to assess the commercial possibilities of countries in Africa and Asia. As discussed in chapter 5, Alexander MacWillie traveled extensively for Heinz and wrote of his trips in the company newsletter. A series of monthly installments that he authored in 1907 is particularly revealing. Part travelogue, part company boosterism, these essays suggest a merging of ideologies similar to what was relayed in the pages of *National Geographic* — affirming cultural stereotypes while also expanding the range of knowledges about the world, "striking a careful balance between the foreign and the familiar."[14] Yet unlike *National Geographic*, Heinz's newsletter was not obliged to promote scientific geography's view of culture as either environmentally or racially determined. MacWillie's discourse moved promiscuously between racist cultural stereotypes and commercial possibilities, as he constantly shifted the terms of his racialized categorizations. His characterizations of China are telling: "Nearing the shore we see huge, ungainly looking junks with tattered sails go lumbering by, their dirty pig-tailed crews lounging over the rails from piles of straw matting and highly odoriferous heaps of dried fish."[15] This stereotype-affirming "opener" to his essay is then followed with descriptions of the countryside and of the streets and shops of Shanghai. The essay closes with statistics as to the trade potential of China ("from a total of 150 million dollars in 1896 the exports and imports increased to over 500 million dollars in 1906"[16]), followed by a description of the future of the country, a future brought about by Western commerce. What is presented by McWillie is a foreign that will soon become familiar — with Western help, of course.

One can see a similar ideology in the travel writings of George Eastman, president and founder of Kodak. His 1896 letter to his mother from Moscow about a commercial fair he had seen in Nijni reveals his view of Russia as a business prospect. After mentioning some of the common racialized stereotypes about the peoples of Asian Russia, he quickly moves to a discussion of commercial potential: "We got a good general idea of it and saw enough to convince us that Russia is advancing rapidly in the arts and manufacturers. It beats the big international exposition at Amsterdam of last year all to pieces even if it was exclusively Russian while that at Amsterdam was international.... When you remember that all this was in a frontier town at the terminus of a railroad in a small place of not over 100,000 and 275 miles from any big city it impresses you with a favorable idea as to what Russia can do."[18]

The term flexible racism helps to make sense of these complicated messages that were infiltrating American homes and consciousnesses, messages in which "others" outside the United States were presented as potentially "white," not as simply frames for the display of commodities, as McClintock would argue. What supported America's "civilization through consumption" was of course an economic system that was increasingly looking to an expanded consumer market to maintain its profitability. American companies neither wanted nor needed colonies that required for their "maintenance" costly military and political support; instead they looked for more consumers. And because America's empire was only "intermittently territorial,"[19] anxieties that centered on commodities and race — that is, anxieties that consumption would break down the boundaries between "us" and "them" — were incidental to the cause of increased profits. In other words, as historian Timothy Burke[20] has shown, in British settler colonies such as South Africa, for example, the fear that commodities would make it possible for black men and women to look and act like white men and women, thus disallowing some of the performance of difference necessary to maintain control, was simply not a primary issue in the American empire outside its political borders. It *was* an issue of course within its borders, as Bobby Wilson has argued so persuasively in his analysis of the relationship between the Jim Crow laws in the American south and the imperatives of commodity capitalism.[21] To put it simply, because American commercial expansion occurred beyond political borders, with real spaces between "us" and "them," the metaphoric spaces could be erased. Because American companies set out to "civilize" through consumption and because those new consumers remained, spatially and discursively, outside the bounds of political citizenship, they could be represented as historical agents in their own right, able to become white through consumption.

This is not to say that American companies refrained from presenting fixed racial difference as an advertising tool. Alongside Singer's and McCormick's promotional images of "others" residing outside the United States were advertisements that represented Native Americans and African Americans in ways that much more cleanly fit McClintock's definition of commodity racism. Native Americans, considered representatives of a dying race, were useful nationalistic reminders of America's distinct, yet remote past, whereas African Americans were thought of as anachronistic degenerates. Neither group, therefore, was considered part of modernity, and neither was able to participate in the community of commodities. They were certainly present in advertising images, but as gimmicks or ornamental sidekicks, not as potential consumers. In a circa 1897 image from an advertising brochure for Ivory soap (see Figure 6.4), Native Americans are depicted in cartoonish, stereotypical form, with soap presented as the magical, civilizing agent, washing away, alongside with "their darkest blots," ignorance and war. This form of commodity racism reinforced the fixed differences that were thought to separate white culture in the United States from Native and African-American cultures.

By the turn of the century, however, American international companies were presenting images of an international and universal community of consumers, images that circulated widely throughout the United States and that worked primarily by loosening some of the fixed differences thought to separate the "races." Yet, this loosening occurred only through a reinforcement of other forms of difference. By focusing on "local" dress and dwellings, for example, the Singer nation cards actively created cultural forms of difference; similarly, McCormick Company showed foreign peoples dressed in local garb,

A NEW DEPARTURE.

Said Uncle Sam: "I will be wise,
And thus the Indian civilize:
Instead of guns, that kill a mile,
Tobacco, lead, and liquor vile,
Instead of serving out a meal,
Or sending Agents out to steal,
I'll give, domestic arts to teach,
A cake of Ivory Soap to each.
Before it flies the guilty stain,
The grease and dirt no more remain;
'Twill change their nature day by day,
And wash their darkest blots away.
They'll turn their bows to fishing-rods,
And bury hatchets under sods,
In wisdom and in worth increase,
And ever smoke the pipe of peace;
For ignorance can never cope
With such a foe as Ivory Soap."

Figure 6.4 "A New Departure," Ivory Soap/Proctor and Gamble advertisement from a pamphlet called "What a Cake of Soap Will Do." (Warshaw Collection of Business Americana, National Museum of American History, Behring Center, Smithsonian Institution)

often using "foreign" animals such as camels to pull their agricultural machinery. Most importantly, spatial differences between "us" and "them" had to be maintained in order to make safe the erasures of difference caused by consumption. As long as "others" remained territorially and politically distant, they could, discursively at least, become like "us." Thus it was important in these images and stories to depict the diversity of countries and regions — to reinscribe spatial borders, to learn the regional geographies of the world.

It is this dual view of the world — one that reasserted at all times geographical difference in order to present, in an unthreatening manner, the loosening of racial difference — that was promoted by these early international companies. It was a worldview that, as we have seen, had precedents in much earlier times but that took on particular meanings as it was translated to fit the needs of an industrial and emerging consumer economy in the last decades of the 19th century. And it was a way of understanding the world that resonated powerfully throughout the first half of the 20th century. Existing alongside the more "scientific" views of racially fixed identities that were expressed in the pages of geography textbooks and magazines, such as *National Geographic*, this flexible racism circulated widely throughout homes and apartments in most parts of the United States. Arguably, its very banality gave it a power over peoples' imaginations that was at least as important as what was presented as "the world" by the official, public organs of geographical knowledge dissemination.

By the time the new commercial geography textbooks appeared in the first decades of the 20th century, therefore, many Americans were already familiar with categorizations of countries that followed an economic and not racial schema. It was a way of seeing the world that had been implied in the many ads and commodities that were scattered throughout their homes and communities. Making this worldview official through its inscription in geography textbooks and school lesson plans strengthened and normalized what had already been popularized. Throughout the 1920s and 1930s, as Susan Schulten and Neil Smith show, this commercial geography shaped American foreign policy, providing scientific legitimation for American commercial expansion.[22] Integral to this worldview were two assumptions: first, that the nations of the world were sorted into a hierarchy based more on access to commodities than on race, and second, that it was only natural that the United States supplied other countries with technical and scientific know-how in the form of those commodities, helping to make them modern.

As scholars have shown, these two assumptions were critical to the discourse of economic development that was formalized after World War II. Gilbert Rist, for example, contends that the "development age" began with "point four" of Truman's 1949 inaugural speech, where the President outlined a program for improving "underdeveloped areas" of the world:[23] "Our main aim should be to help the free peoples of the world, through their own efforts, to produce more food, more clothing, more materials for housing, and more mechanical power to lighten their burdens."[24] This notion of using American technical and economic expertise to help other areas of the world, to everyone's mutual benefit, was, as Rist suggests, nothing particularly new; rather, it "synthesized a number of ideas that were obviously in line with the Zeitgeist."[25] What *was* new according to Rist was that this statement of goals put together a way of "conceiving international relations"[26] that was novel in two ways. First, instead of the hierarchical view of the world implied within the colonial world order — one that fixed nations into positions either of colony or colonizer — this new order conceived of a world where every nation was theoretically equal to each other, if not yet in fact equal. In Rist's words, "Now, however, 'underdeveloped' and 'developed' were members of a single family: the one might be lagging a little behind the other, but they could always hope to catch up."[27] Second, within the new world order, underdevelopment was seen as a natural condition, one that just happened, while development was an historical condition, one that could be brought about by human action. Thus, the developed countries could bring development to other countries in the form of economic and technical assistance. Here is how Truman put it: "Greater production is the key to prosperity and peace. And the key to greater production is a wider and more vigorous application of modern scientific and technical knowledge. Only by helping the least fortunate of its members to help themselves can the human family achieve the decent, satisfying life that is the right of all people."[28]

Compare this to how McCormick Harvesting Machine Company presented the world, almost 65 years earlier: "In the grand march of human progress which distinguishes the present age above all others, agricultural machinery occupies a prominent position, being second to none in its important bearing on the well-being of society. It has released the farmer from the drudgery of life, almost miraculously increased the production of food, and so far reduced its cost that the human family to-day is better fed and better clothed than at any time in all its previous history."[29] The "decent, satisfying life" of Truman's "human family" was, according to McCormick, already being achieved through the sale of agricultural machinery, as it had decreased the "drudgery of life" and increased the "production of food" for the "human family." The ideological foundations and racial beliefs of Rist's "development age," it seems, have a rather long and complex history, a history that needs to include American commodity culture of the late 19th century.

I do not mean to suggest that the complex set of ideas and practices that constitute the term "development" began in this time and place. As many scholars have pointed out, development grew out of ideas that far predated this time period and developed at least as much in reaction to the West as emanating out from it.[30] But I do want to suggest that the nexus of ideas that comprises this flexible form of racism is important to what Michael Watts has called the "archaeology of development" — that is, the search into the historical, geographic, and cultural sites of its production.[31] What I have argued here is that the stories that late 19th century, U.S.-based international companies were telling Americans about the world constituted one of those sites. And this site is particularly interesting for several reasons. First, in distinction to what have been traditionally noted as the sites of "development" stories — public policy documents, political philosophies, "formalized" scholarship — these stories were produced by agents of commodity capitalism. In other words, these development stories were directly tied to the interests that they served. As a result, therefore, the links between industrial capitalism and the production of development discourse were made transparent. Second, as pieces of commercial culture, these stories circulated widely throughout the United States. As we have seen in this book, trade cards, catalogs, and other forms of advertisement and promotion were offered either free of charge or purchased at an affordable rate; they were dispersed through the commercial networks of popular magazines, expositions, door-to-door salesmen, and small retail shops; and some, as was evident in the case of McCormick catalogs, were printed in several languages. Third, many of these documents were long lived because, as aesthetic objects, they were often collected and displayed in homes and in scrapbooks. As a result, these "development" stories popularized messages of a flexible racism, making natural the idea that economics differentiated peoples of the world as much as race and that American products could potentially make the peoples of the world all alike.

What I have presented in this book are just some of the many and diverse advertising images and discourses that circulated, shaping subjectivities within the spaces of middle-class American homes. My analysis here suggests how an explicitly commercial outlook created and reiterated a particular image of "others," forming a hierarchical view of the world based on access to commodities and not simply race and laying the foundations for a modern discourse of development, for a belief, that is, in the transformative powers of Western reason and technology. Alexander MacWillie's assessment of Japan might well serve to characterize commercial imperial knowledges in general: "Japan of the Nineteenth Century is rapidly passing away, and Japan of the Twentieth Century is developing to an extent not even surpassed by the growth of our own great republic."[32] Commercial imperial knowledges, it seems, were all about assessing the growth potential of the world's regions.

The global spread of American-style commercial culture has continued almost unabatedly throughout the 20th century, and with it, cultural geographies of imperialism have been reshaped and reinforced. My concentration on commodities and markets has precluded analysis of the world of production and labor that is such a major component of America's economic dominance today, but the cultural "life" of commodities still resonates powerfully in the representational world of the early 21st century. And although the myriad causes and effects of globalization are hotly contested,[33] and some see its contemporary manifestation as qualitatively distinct from globalizing processes in the late 19th and early 20th centuries,[34] I hope my analyses have promoted a recognition of the historical linkages as well as the disjunctures between the early 21st century and the early 20th century. In this way, my work would contribute to an "awareness of multiplicity" — an awareness that the ideologies and practices of one time and place do not simply disappear but "coexist with new ways of thinking and living" and can reappear at much later times in different forms.[35]

As I have suggested throughout this book, the categories of difference that dominated the representations created and reiterated by the five American companies I examined built on discourses that dated from the early 18th century, and those categories of difference in turn were revised and retrofitted into narratives of progress that characterized the worldview of late 19th century and early 20th century American commercial expansion. Different imperial situations, then, reiterated and circulated different categories of difference. The notion that racial identity and stages along the civilizational hierarchy were not fixed but instead malleable was not particular to America's era of informal imperialism (as noted earlier, they have deep historical roots, and were widespread throughout parts of Europe), but it was more consistent and more dominant within this particular time and space. And the stories that these ideas narrate shed new light on the multiple and complex historical relationships between the United States and its economic empire, highlighting another aspect of the "messy, mixed-up, interconnected nature of histories, geographies and identities"[36] that comprise the present-day imperial and global world.

When middle-class women read their popular magazines and saw ads for sewing machines, pickles, and cameras, they were participants in a form of cosmopolitanism shaped by an emerging American empire, an empire based on commercial expansion that was legitimized through racism. But that racism was different from the "scientific" racism that was circulating at the same time. It was a flexible racism — a fluid hierarchy in which commodities could, discursively at least, erase difference. It was an ideology that made it appear as if the peoples of the world could be united in a family of common consumption, albeit a patriarchal family, with the United States positioned as the masculine producer, and the rest of the world positioned as the feminine consumer. Thus, flexible racism made it seem only natural that the United States would dominate the world's commercial networks.

Endnotes

1. Susan Schulten, *The Geographical Imagination in America, 1880–1950* (Chicago: University of Chicago Press, 2001), 13.
2. Ibid.
3. Gilbert Rist, *The History of Development from Western Origins to Global Faith* (London: Zed Books, 1999).
4. Anne McClintock, *Imperial Leather: Race, Gender, and Sexuality in the Colonial Contest* (New York: Routledge, 1995), 33.
5. Ibid., 34.
6. Kristin Hoganson, "Cosmopolitan Domesticity: Importing the American Dream, 1865–1920," *American Historical Review*, 107 (2002): 55–83.
7. Ibid., 60.
8. For the best discussion of how ideas of evolution and millennial thought combined with the flexible discourse of civilization, see Gail Bederman's *Manliness and Civilization: A Cultural History of Gender and Race in the United States, 1880–1917* (Chicago: University of Chicago Press, 1995), particularly chapter 1.
9. I am compressing here into one sentence a complex genealogy of thought. For a rich discussion of the linkages between turn-of-the-century notions of civilization and the post–World War II discourse of development, see Rist's *The History of Development from Western Origins to Global Faith*.
10. Roxann Wheeler, *The Complexion of Race: Categories of Difference in Eighteenth-Century British Culture* (Philadelphia: University of Pennsylvania Press, 2000).
11. Ibid., 6.
12. Ibid., 39.
13. McCormick Catalog, 1900.
14. Schulten (2001), 175.
15. Alexander MacWillie, "Impressions of the Orient," *The 57 Life, 3*, 2 (May, 1907): 4.
16. Ibid., 5.
17. Eastman letters, 1896, Eastman house archives, Rochester, NY.
18. John A. Agnew and Joanne Sharp, "America, Frontier Nation: From Abstract Space to Worldly Place," in *American Space/American Place: Geographies of the Contemporary United States*, eds. John A. Agnew and Jonathan Smith, (New York: Routledge, 2002), 89.

19. Timothy Burke, *Lifebuoy Men, Lux Women: Commodification, Consumption, and Cleanliness in Modern Zimbabwe* (Durham, NC: Duke University Press, 1996).

20. Wilson argues that the ability of mass consumption to dissolve "difference" threatened white southerners whose response was to enact what became known as "Jim Crow laws," thereby legally enforcing "difference" in the form of spatial segregation. See Bobby Wilson, "Race in Commodity Exchange and Consumption: Separate but Equal," *Annals of the Association of American Geographers, 95* (2005).

21. Schulten (2001); Neil Smith, *American Empire: Roosevelt's Geographer and the Prelude to Globalization* (Berkeley: University of California Press, 2003).

22. Rist (1999), 71.

23. From Public Papers of the Presidents, Harry Truman, Year 1949, U.S. Printing Office, 1964, January 20, 114–115, Quoted in ibid., 71.

24. Rist (1999), 72.

25. Ibid., 72.

26. Ibid., 74.

27. Quoted in ibid., 72.

28. McCormick Catalog, 1885.

29. See Albert O. Hirschman, *Rival Views of Market Society and Other Recent Essays* (New York: Viking Press, 1986).

30. Michael Watts, "Alternative Modern — Development as Cultural Geography," in *Handbook of Cultural Geography*, ed. Kay Anderson et al., (Thousand Oaks, CA: Sage Publications, 2003), 436.

31. MacWillie (1907), 4.

32. Paul Hirst and Grahame Thompson, *Globalization in Question: The International Economy and the Possibilities of Governance* (Malden,MA: Blackwell Publishers, 1999).

33. Michael Hardt and Antonio Negri, *Empire* (Cambridge, MA: Harvard University Press, 2000).

34. Wheeler (2000), 39.

35. Ian Cook and Michelle Harrison, "Cross over Food: Re-materializing Postcolonial Geographies," *Transactions of the Institute of British Geographers, 28* (2003): 297.

Index